VOICE OF A VICTIM

Overcoming the Generational Curse
of Sexual Abuse and Incest

ERICA JANELLE

Erica has transitioned from being a victim various forms of trauma into an astute entrepreneur and owner of three successful businesses which includes Overcoming Abuse Through Healing Inc. (OATH). OATH Is a non-profit that she launched to assist victims of trauma. She took her personal trauma and used her pain to birth her purpose and help others navigate through their pain and trauma. It brings her great delight to see people succeed in relationships, career goals, financial success, and spiritual growth. Having had her share of the despair of toxic relationships, she has become more insightful, resourceful, and passionate about herself. Erica now uses her experience to encourage self-love and healing.

A remarkable coach and mentor, Erica hopes to help people bring their goals and dreams to fruition. She finds it rewarding to use her experience from single parenting and juggling career responsibilities, to motivate individuals to have a more streamlined relationship with their career. Erica is set to use her knowledge to propel, inspire, and guide you on your journey of success. In addition to her coaching career, she brings over 15 years of experience in Human Resources field and holds an MBA and a Masters in Human resources.

Copyright © 2022 Erica Janelle LLC.

All rights reserved. This book or any portion thereof may not be reproduced or used in any manner whatsoever without the express written permission of the publisher except for the use of brief quotations in a book review.

Table of Contents

Introduction – Exposing the Reality 1

Chapter 1 – My Initial Exposure 5

Chapter 2 – The First Time 13

Chapter 3 – New Abusers, Different Type of Sexual Abuse 23

Chapter 4 – To Move Forward, Sometimes You Have to Take a Step Back 31

Chapter 5 – How My Past Sexual Abuse Caused Me to Choose Wrong 41

Chapter 6 – How the Past Was Revealed and Would be Useful in My Future . 47

Chapter 7 – The Most Painful Part of This Journey 57

Chapter 8 – Getting Justice Using the Legal System 69

Chapter 9 – The Legal Process Continued 75

Chapter 10 – The Beginning of the Healing Process 83

— INTRODUCTION —
Exposing the Reality

It's a topic that causes a myriad of emotions: sadness, anger, pain, fear, embarrassment, and shame. It's a topic that no one wants to talk about and oftentimes people refuse to discuss because of the pain it causes. I'm talking about molestation and, more specifically, incest that takes place in families on a daily basis. This topic is one that has rocked my family for generations, and, frankly, one that I am still ashamed to discuss because of how much pain it dredges up in my heart and the embarrassment associated with it. My biggest concern is my fear of hurting the people I love and cherish deeply.

As I write, my heart is racing because it hurts to actually say this out loud and admit that this is my reality. Putting actual words to this topic makes it real and an issue that I can no longer bury. I am choosing to confront this issue head-on so that I can continue my journey to healing and helping others heal. The simple fact is that molestation and incest are topics no one wants to discuss. It's like opening Pandora's box—inviting a subject that for years your family held in secret, or an issue that everyone knew was happening but was too afraid and ashamed to discuss, to be openly discussed.

Like many families, my family doesn't know how to discuss this topic openly. To be clear, my intention is in no way to point the finger at or cause guilt for family members who did not know how to deal with the issue, but rather to expose an area that needs to be discussed so that generational curses can be broken, strongholds can be destroyed, and generational healing can begin. Additionally, my purpose is to focus on *my* story and *my* personal journey rather than to share the specifics of my family members' journeys. Due to the sensitivity of this topic, I am very mindful not to delve deeply into others' stories and subsequently create another way to rob victims of telling their own stories, but rather to expose some of the history of the issue of incest and sexual abuse that has rocked my family as well as so many others. While it is virtually impossible to discuss the origins of the issue of incest without mentioning how this has affected my family for generations, I want to assure my readers that I spoke with my family members and received permission before including even an inkling of their personal stories.

There are a ton of mixed emotions that this book had and will cause. When I mentioned that I was writing this book to some family members, it caused mixed emotions for many. Some family members thought that I should not write this book because of the shame and embarrassment it would bring upon our family. Others wanted me to speak to the family before revealing this issue. My sole purpose for writing this book is to give voice to the issue and reveal that this is an issue that many people, unfortunately, have experienced.

Because of the shame and fear that sexual abuse and incest causes, many people are either told to keep it a secret or have chosen on their own to keep it a secret. Others have chosen to sweep it under the rug and pretend that it never occurred. In my family, we would continue to go to family gatherings, laughing and joking and pretending that everything was okay while the victims were forced to be around the perpetrators. I felt compelled to write this book because I want to give voice to the victims and break the stigma behind discussing this sensitive subject. I want to banish the sense of shame and fear that this crime has caused, and I want to create a safe space so victims can know that they are not alone.

Most importantly, I feel a sense of duty to break the cycle and teach our children that this cycle ends here and now. My sincere prayer is that those of you reading this book will, first of all, realize that you are not alone and, secondly, understand that you have what it takes to be the change in your family and break and destroy this generational curse. You are stronger than you know, and when you don't have the strength, God will be your strength and healer! I pray for God's peace and healing to provide breakthroughs all over the world and change and impact society!

— CHAPTER 1 —

My Initial Exposure

I want to preface this chapter by saying that I have blocked certain periods of my childhood out of my mind, likely due to the level of trauma. This is not unusual for victims of sexual abuse; psychologically, it is a defense mechanism to protect the victim from having an emotional break. While I am not a therapist or psychologist, I have been in therapy for many years, and therapy has helped me to recognize that this is quite common for victims of various forms of trauma.

My very first memories of sexual abuse came from two of my female cousins when I was around five or six years of age. They were children as well, maybe five or six years older than me. Looking back, I realize that they, too, were likely being touched or exposed to sexual things early on because of the sexual acts they would make me perform on them and ones that they would perform on me. This is so heartbreaking because they were so young themselves, too young, in fact, to understand the depravity and hurt they caused. I remember looking up to my cousins and older siblings, wanting to be like them. These cousins would often come to our house to hang out with us. As an innocent child, I didn't understand inappropriate touch, nor did I understand why my older cousins would want to harm me. While I knew it felt wrong the first time it happened, I was confused and sad all at the same time. We were playing hide-and-seek, and I think one of my sisters was "it." We all ran and hid in our respective hiding spots. One of my cousins ran with me and hid where I was hiding. I asked my cousin why she would hide in my spot because it would be easier for us to be found.

"Because I couldn't find anywhere else to go," she said forcefully. I didn't think much of it at first. We had found a quiet spot in the living room where we children were forbidden to play, so I figured it would be hard for my sibling to find me. Minutes went by, and we could hear the other siblings laughing and screaming as, one by one, they were being found. I just knew I had found the perfect space.

Suddenly, my cousin lifted up her shirt and told me to lick and suck on her breasts. I remember being confused and afraid at the same time, asking her why she would have me do that.

"You'd better do it, or I'm going to beat you up and tell your mom that you hit me," she said. As a six-year-old, I was terrified of my big cousin, and at that age, I was super sensitive and would cry at the drop of a dime, which all of my family knew and would often tease me for. It goes without saying that I did it, and it seemed like a lifetime before we heard my siblings and my other cousin asking where we both were.

She quickly put her shirt down and said, "We're right here."

I remember feeling both sad and terrified. I felt filthy and disgusting because, after all, I was the one who had performed the sexual act on her. In my six-year-old mind, I thought I had done something wrong, not realizing I was a victim.

I don't know how I managed to move on and pretend I was okay in front of everyone else, but I do remember feeling an overwhelming sense of fear and shame. That particular night, my cousins didn't stay the night with us, as they would often do, and I must've felt a sense of relief. I remember wanting to tell my oldest sister, who was around the ages of my cousins, but I feared she wouldn't believe me. This was when the cycle of keeping the sexual abuse I experienced a secret began.

This is very common among victims of trauma. From what I've learned and from my personal experience, victims often keep molestation and sexual abuse a secret because they are ashamed and are often intimidated and threatened by the oppressors to keep the acts of sexual deviance quiet. Honestly, I believe this is why many cases of generational sexual abuse continue.

From my personal experience, I know that children often blame themselves for sexual abuse, thinking they did something wrong to allow this behavior. Even more common, they feel so much shame that it is often easier just to bury the secret. In addition to feeling that sense of shame and fear, I also loved my cousin and didn't want to see her get into trouble. I feared that I would somehow be viewed as the bad guy if my cousins were no longer allowed to visit us. The confusion and mixed emotions this one incident caused were the reasons I kept it a secret. It's hard to imagine the level of pressure children face on a daily basis when dealing with this issue.

A few years ago, when I began speaking about my personal experience with a family member, that family member told me I was overreacting by calling it abuse because we were both children and it's normal for children to explore. I was appalled by this response. While children are naturally sexually curious, demanding and forcing someone to perform sexual acts on another is not normal. Not only is this behavior not normal, it's also not acceptable at any age to force sex on another person. My feeling is that this mentality that it is natural is why the issue of sexual abuse and incest are so prevalent in society and almost viewed as acceptable behavior.

Let me make it very clear: it was not only WRONG, it was also unnatural for my cousin to want to explore sex with her six-year-old female cousin when she was no older than eleven years old herself. I can't help but think that she was probably molested by someone herself based on the forcefulness with which she made me perform the acts on her. Again, I want to make it clear that I don't blame her. I know she was just a child herself and probably did not know the extent of damage her actions caused.

While people's opinions may vary about the severity of this initial sexual act, it affected me and literally opened the door for me to become exposed and vulnerable for additional instances of sexual abuse, which I will discuss in further chapters. I want to be very clear that I don't hold any ill feelings toward my cousins, even though we haven't spoken in many years. It's very likely that they, too, were molested, and my desire is to bring healing by exposing this issue within families, especially within the Black community.

Before moving on to my next point, I feel led to share this. There is this belief around molestation, rape, and other forms of sexual abuse that the experiences of some are not as severe as others, devaluing that person's experience and therefore creating this perception that one person's experience is not as traumatic as someone else's. Please understand that trauma comes in many forms, and just because one person's experience may not seem as traumatic as another's, the fact is that many people carry this shame and never speak up against it because they fear how others will perceive them. I feel compelled to share this message to those who try to minimize the validity of their experience and encourage them to speak their truth and never let anyone silence them from doing so. For everyone struggling with guilt when it comes to acknowledging whether or not the sexual abuse they experienced was severe, please know that no matter how big or small, no one has the right to subject you to sexual acts without your permission and consent. Additionally, no child should be exposed to sexual behaviors or acts because children are not physically, psychologically, or emotionally mature enough to even understand sexuality at such a young and tender age.

We are often taught in the Black community to ignore, keep silent about, and never express the things that are going on within the household. Whether the trauma is due to alcoholism, drug addiction, verbal or physical abuse, or anything else, children are told never to discuss what happens behind closed doors. While I believe there is a certain level of discretion needed to avoid airing all of your dirty laundry for anyone to hear, parents and guardians have to be mindful not to create an environment where children are afraid to tell their parents or someone they trust the truth. It is my sincere belief that children should not be put in a position where they are responsible for keeping family secrets. In addition, I believe children are often forced to grow up too quickly because of the things they have been exposed to in their households instead of being able to walk in the bliss of freedom that comes with childhood. As responsible adults, we should do our due diligence to create an environment for children that provides them with a safe space to openly share the things they are experiencing, including being able to tell a trusted adult about sexual abuse that may be happening.

When children have this safe space to openly share, and, more specifically, when parents and/or trusted loved ones speak on these issues, it creates an environment where children will more likely feel comfortable to share any sexual misconduct that they are exposed to.

This brings me to my next point. Families that take the time to have conversations openly discussing sexual abuse, inappropriate touch, and sexual advances create an environment where children will feel safe discussing these issues because it's not such a taboo subject, but rather one that the children are familiar with. This is so important. I think we must take an active stance to overcome the fear of talking about uncomfortable topics and understand that the failure to discuss such topics will often cause more severe repercussions than the initial discomfort of talking to children about these issues.

I recall many times in my childhood when my mother and aunts would speak to me and my siblings about inappropriate touch and how to be aware of our surroundings when in the presence of adults. Unfortunately, growing up in a household with several family members who suffered from severe alcoholism, my grandfather and great-aunts and uncles would often have a lot of men around the house whom they would drink with, and as a result, we children had to pay close attention to being around these people. There were many times when my grandfather was passed out drunk, and his associates had plenty of opportunity to make inappropriate comments or even engage in inappropriate touch with us. Having the conversations about what to look out for made us more vigilant and aware of our surroundings, and it afforded us the chance to go outside and play when those instances happened. I also credit my oldest sister for protecting us younger children. She made sure we were never left alone with those individuals and was damn near willing to fight anyone who tried to cause us harm or said or did anything inappropriate around us. She feared that they would try to take advantage of us while my grandfather was unconscious. Knowing about the possibility of sexual assault, she felt the need to protect us.

While having open discussions as a family did not prevent the sexual abuse in my life, they eventually made it easier for me to tell those I trusted about the sexual abuse that happened to me. I honestly believe that my experiences could have been even more severe had I not had the discussions early on with my family. I am forever grateful to my mother, who, despite her own severe sexual abuse and experiences, tried her best to protect us as her children. She went through so much abuse and trauma herself, but she did the best she could. When I think of my major motivation for writing this book, it would have to be to give voice and retribution to my mother and my children. I have a special love and sense of protection over my mother, and as her child, I am giving voice to her, despite her being silenced from sharing her own experiences her entire life. We spoke very candidly about my desire to write this book, and she said that she gave me permission to share the generational issues with sexual abuse and incest because she recognizes the higher good that we are doing in helping others to overcome these generational curses.

— CHAPTER 2 —

The First Time

My siblings and I grew up in a very crowded home and were often exposed to a high volume of individuals coming in and out of our home. We looked forward to the summertime when we would spend a month or two with our aunts in New York. It was a time for us to enjoy just being kids, and as an added bonus, we often had the opportunity to act and sing in our aunt's production company. As a family that is heavily involved in the arts, we were exposed to the arts from a very early age. When I was around the age of ten or eleven, we were told that my aunt's new husband, who was from Pakistan, was driving to Maryland to come pick us up. At this time, there were only four of us living with my mom: my oldest sister, my second sister, my twin brother, and myself. My youngest sister was living with her dad in Germany.

We were extremely excited about this road trip, and we were going to split our time between the three aunts' houses. The first few days, we would be with my aunt Mary and her husband, Thomas, and then spend the next few days with my other two aunts who lived together, Gina and Trish. The first night was exciting, and all the girls piled up on the sofa bed in the living room while my twin brother made a pallet on the floor. The first few days, our uncle Thomas was fun and cool to be around. He made us feel comfortable and welcomed in their home. He would even cook some of his signature dishes from his culture and watch television with us.

Often, when it comes to predators, they want to create a sense of comfort with children. They build this sense of rapport and trust so the children are more willing to let their guard down. This is exactly what our uncle did with us girls. The only one he didn't try to manipulate was my oldest sister because she was a teenager and was definitely not one who could be easily influenced.

One night, my sisters and I were sleeping on the sofa bed, and late in the night, I woke up to him coming up behind me on the sofa bed and lying next to me. The first time this happened, I was terrified and confused. I remember asking him why he was in the bed with us, and he said he was just making sure we were okay. He then told me to be quiet so that I didn't wake up my sisters. This was the first time I felt a sense of fear around him because his tone was very stern and totally different from any tone he had had with me before.

I remember lying still in the bed, trying not to even breathe too hard. During this initial time, he touched me on my body and made me touch him. He would press his penis against my butt. His very touch made me feel nauseous. He was extremely hairy, and I was grossed out touching him. This initial interaction probably only lasted a few minutes, but it felt like hours. He then got up and went back to his bedroom with my aunt, who was sound asleep. I cried myself to sleep that night, too afraid to wake up my sisters and tell them what had happened to me.

The next morning, he pretended that nothing had happened and attempted to be the same caring, fun uncle he was before, but my view of him was forever changed. I felt an overwhelming desire to tell my oldest sister, whom I always viewed as my protector, but I remember feeling a sense of fear that he would hurt me or even make us leave and end our summer vacation early. I didn't want to be responsible for ruining everyone's vacation. Also, at this point, there was nothing more than him just touching me, and I didn't feel that it was severe enough to cause any drama. As a person who has healed and grown, it makes me more upset that, at that age, I felt compelled to become a martyr in a sense, putting myself to the side and considering everyone else rather than the things I was being exposed to. We were scheduled to go to my other aunts' house, which helped me be at ease, knowing that I wouldn't have to deal with this for a while.

The next few days, I was able to get my mind off of that event because we were busy enjoying time with my other aunts, who were keeping us occupied helping in their theatre productions. This was something that provided a much-needed escape from being under Uncle Thomas's eye; however, the fear I felt about returning to their home was always there, under the surface. Regardless, at this time, I was able to go back to my jovial self and enjoy the opportunity to be a part of my aunts' productions, go to new restaurants, and enjoy other activities, such as going to my aunt's job where she worked at night.

Even though I was able to temporarily get my mind off of what had transpired between me and my uncle, I knew it was going to be short-lived because, eventually, we were going to return to my aunt's house, which ultimately meant I would have to be around my uncle. I remember feeling nervous about going back but hoped that event would be a one-time deal. I thought that if I stayed close to my siblings and didn't spend any time with my uncle alone, I would be safe.

Everything was normal when we arrived. We were laughing, joking, playing games, and listening to my aunt's collection of Whitney Houston records, who was my all-time favorite artist and who ultimately sparked my passion for singing and performing. My sisters and I would have singing contests to see who could sing her music the best. I enjoyed our time at the house during the day because my aunt and uncle were at work and I knew I would be safe. That first night, I convinced my twin brother and sisters to stay up and watch movies. I knew that if we were having a movie night, it meant we would try to stay up all night. The plan was to stay together and stay awake so that he would be less likely to come in the living room. We stayed up until we could see the sun coming up, and, fortunately, my uncle did not come out of his bedroom all night. I remember feeling so relieved, and I convinced myself that maybe, just maybe, the sexual abuse wouldn't happen again.

The sense of relief definitely helped me believe that things would be the way they always were. We went on for a few more days without any incidents. I felt it was safe to let my guard down, which I did. The fear, while still slightly present, no longer consumed my thoughts. It was bedtime, and I remember feeling completely safe until we found out that my aunt was not going to be home all night. I can't remember where she was this particular night, but I remember feeling in the pit of my stomach that this night was going to be different, and not in a good way.

I stayed up with my twin brother watching television until he fell asleep. I was tired and wanted to sleep, but I was afraid to fall into a deep sleep because if I was wide awake, he would not be so bold to climb into bed with me. My sister who was a year older than me was still awake, and we were up talking and laughing quietly so as to not wake my oldest sister and my brother who were lying near us. Eventually, my sister fell asleep, and then I did as well. I don't know how long I was asleep before I heard a noise coming from the doorway. As a light sleeper, it is not unusual for me to wake up after hearing a noise. I remember wanting to keep my eyes closed and be very still in case he was planning to come in the bed next to me.

Eventually, my dreaded nightmare happened. He stood there for a while without moving. I figured he was making sure my siblings were sleeping. I clinched my eyes closed tight to brace myself for what I knew was about to happen. He climbed onto the sofa bed next to me. I can't remember all of the details, but he was not wearing a shirt, and all I can picture even now is how hairy he was. I remember feeling sick to my stomach feeling all of the hair on his body. He climbed in behind me and rubbed his penis against my butt. He put one hand over my mouth to ensure that I wouldn't scream or wake anyone. I remember him whispering in my ear not to make a sound. He then took his penis out of his pajama pants and rubbed it against my butt. I could feel him getting more and more erect as he did so. With one hand on my mouth and the other on his penis, he began to slowly insert his penis into my anus. I was completely terrified and afraid. The first time he placed the tip of his penis in my anus, it was painful, but not as painful as it could've been had he placed more of his penis inside me. I knew that if I made any noise, he would hurt me.

He slowly removed his hand from my mouth and proceeded to place his hand inside my vagina. He started with just one finger and then proceeded to place more fingers inside me. He continued to rub his penis against my butt while keeping his fingers inside me. He then removed his fingers from the front of my vagina and entered the same fingers inside my vagina from the back. He slowly entered the tip of his penis inside me. I remember jumping and making a noise to indicate I was in pain. He then stopped trying to penetrate me vaginally for a moment before proceeding to enter his penis in me with more force but more slowly. I could tell he could feel my body trembling, as I was crying uncontrollably but trying my best not to make a sound. I knew if I woke my siblings, I would be in trouble.

He continued to force himself inside me but was careful enough not to break my hymen. As I look back on the incident, I realize he must've done this before because he only caused a small amount of bleeding. He then whispered in my ear to get up and follow him to his bedroom. With tears in my eyes, I begged him to let me stay in the room with my siblings. He then said for me to follow him. He tried to reassure me that he wasn't going to hurt me. He walked out of the living room where we slept and told me to meet him in his bedroom.

As I was about to get up from the sofa bed and go into the bedroom, my sister woke up. She saw the look on my face, and I told her that he had touched me. I was too ashamed to tell her the full details at the time, as I feared she wouldn't believe me. Despite this fear, she told me to stay in the bed with her and to not go in the bedroom. She said if he came back, she would come with me to make sure I was safe. I remember feeling so relieved that she was there and that I didn't have to be afraid anymore.

Some of the memories are a bit fuzzy, but I remember feeling so stupid, or even that I had done this to myself by not screaming and waking up my sisters or my brother who was across the room. As I have healed and come to terms with this situation, I realize that children often blame themselves for not telling someone or for not screaming.

However, what I've learned over the course of time is that predators use their influence and position in a child's life to deceive them. Especially if it's a family member or close friend, they use their position to deceive the child and make them feel comfortable, and even as if the child asked for it. They use their position to manipulate and deceive vulnerable and innocent children.

I moved closer to my sister on the sofa bed, and as we were talking, he came back in the room and told us both to go to his bedroom. My sister looked at me, and she and I both went to his bedroom. (I often wonder what would've happened if we had told him no.) He told my sister and I to lie on each side of him. He wanted us both to rub on his chest. Again, the details are a bit fuzzy, but I recall the energy being different with my uncle when my sister and I were in the bedroom with him. I don't remember him touching us as much; it was more him making us touch him. I don't believe he attempted to penetrate us when we both were in the bedroom, but I can't say for sure.

It took me years to recall the details of this and other events because I had blocked many of those memories. It was through several years of counseling and therapy that these memories were able to resurface. I often tell some of my coaching clients that it is completely normal to fail to remember some of your memories of trauma. I believe that our minds block some of those memories intentionally in order to keep us from losing our minds. I don't think I will ever recall all of the memories from my childhood. To be honest, recalling all of my childhood trauma wouldn't even benefit me at this point. I am more focused on healing and moving forward than going too far back into my past. While doing the work to overcome your past is necessary, it can't be your primary focus. You must focus your energy on moving forward as a healed individual.

I can't tell you how long we were in the bedroom with him, but it seemed like an eternity, and I also don't recall how we ended back up in the living room. I remember talking to my sister the next morning about how we needed to tell my other aunt and my oldest sister what happened. She initially didn't feel that it was necessary to tell anyone because, from her perspective, he didn't "rape" us. I then told her in more detail what he did to me prior to her waking up. She then agreed that we couldn't tell Aunt Mary, but we could tell our other aunts. When we spoke to my oldest sister, she agreed that we should make sure that Aunt Gina knew about it and didn't tell Aunt Mary until we were scheduled to leave Aunt Mary and Uncle Thomas's house.

We decided to call Aunt Gina and tell her about the incident that happened with me, Uncle Thomas, and my sister. I never told her the details of what happened when he was alone with me, but I did tell her how he asked me and my sister to come to the bedroom and how he wanted us to rub on him. I begged Aunt Gina not to tell Aunt Mary. She said that she would speak with Aunt Mary but would not let her know which one of us had told her about the incident. I remember feeling fear, embarrassment, and shame.

As with most victims of child molestation, I blamed myself and thought it was something I had done wrong to make that situation happen to me. I will never forget that feeling. All I could think about was how it was my fault that my aunt would have to be devastated by this news and how it would ruin her life. I didn't think about how I was made to feel, just the guilt and shame over what my aunt would feel. The mere thought of causing her pain made me want to go back to Baltimore early just so I wouldn't have to witness her pain and anguish. Aunt Gina assured me that she wouldn't tell Aunt Mary about this until we left. She would make sure we stayed with her and Aunt Trish through the remainder of our time in New York.

The time finally came for us to leave New York. It was bittersweet, as I always enjoyed the time with my aunts and getting to act, sing, and dance in their plays. I was exposed to many cultural differences that helped shape my love and appreciation for many of the things I value today. I knew that, despite all of those wonderful times, I would still have to face the reality of what happened between my uncle and me and my sister. I could not ignore the guilt I felt for potentially being the cause of my aunt's marriage falling apart. This was more of a worry for me than my own safety because, as a child, I wanted to protect her from the hurt she would feel once she knew the truth. I always looked up to my aunts and would never want to disappoint or cause any of them pain.

My uncle drove us back to Maryland, and I knew the ride home would probably feel like the longest ride of my life and possibly the most uncomfortable. But it had to be done. I vaguely remember trying to act as normal as possible so that I didn't send up any red flags to my aunt. I was quiet most of the way home and tried to avoid eye contact with my uncle. We eventually made it home, and I remember feeling like I just wanted to be normal and move forward. When we got back home, I did not tell my mother and urged my aunt not to tell her either; I was so afraid of what my mom would do. I just wanted to forget about it and move on as if nothing had happened. I justified this mindset by telling myself that since my hymen wasn't broken during the incident, I was still a virgin, and no one would ever have to know. I forced myself to believe that it wasn't a big deal and I should just move on, and that's exactly what I did.

Time moved on, and I remember getting a call either later that year or the next that my aunt and uncle were getting divorced and he was moving back to Pakistan. This made me feel very sad because the memories of that night that I tried so hard to bury came back to haunt me again. I immediately felt responsible for ruining their marriage. Even though no one ever told me the reason for the divorce, I knew it was my fault. I blamed myself and convinced myself that my aunt hated me because of it. From that moment on, I no longer wanted to talk about any of my experiences with anyone. As a result, I pretty much withdrew from people and began to bury myself in my church and disconnect myself from my family.

— CHAPTER 3 —

New Abusers, Different Type of Sexual Abuse

My mother met this guy who was a few years younger than her. He would later on move in with us and ultimately father two of my younger brothers. When we first met him, my siblings and I liked him because he was funny and seemed to be very cool with us. I remember sitting at the dining room table with him, my uncle (a different uncle and my absolute favorite uncle), and my mom while he taught us how to play cards. My uncle and this guy were friends, and our uncle lived with us at the time. We would play spades, tonk, and other card games. It was a really cool time for us, having someone who was fun to be around and who, at the beginning, made my mom happy.

Over the course of time, he moved in with us, and things started to change. His relationship with my mom was strained, and they began to argue a lot because he couldn't hold down a job. Instead of working, he would have his best friend and cousin, a known drug addict, over to play card games, smoke, and drink. This put a huge strain on their relationship, and we would often hear bad arguments and even physical fights between them. As their relationship began to worsen, he started partying with his cousin and friends in the basement, and they began to abuse drugs together. My siblings and I were little private detectives. We would go down to the basement after they were gone and hide their drug paraphernalia and collect our evidence in order to present it to our mom. Beyond all of that, my sisters and I noticed that he looked at us differently, in a sexual way. He would drill little holes in the door to watch us while we showered. He would steal our underwear and use them to masturbate. At this point, my sister was a teenager and had had her fill of living in sexually abusive situations. She was more bold to not only confront him, but to protect us as her siblings.

One day, she made a decision to present all of the drug evidence to my mom since the sexual perversions had not caused her to put him out of our home. We grabbed his crack pipes, pornography, and whatever other evidence we found and showed it to my mother. I don't remember her initial response, but I do remember she was pregnant with one of my little brothers at the time. They stayed together for several years but eventually went their separate ways after my two brothers were born.

During this time, we were introduced to a church and a wonderful environment that took us in like family. I immersed myself in this environment because it gave me a sense of purpose and safety. My spiritual growth and journey started there and were the catalysts for getting into coaching, mentoring, music, and using all of my gifts and talents.

I found myself spending more time in the church than my other family members, and as a result, I became very close with the leaders of that ministry. Because my family was so poor and my mom was a single mom with many kids, the leaders would pitch in and buy us clothing, school supplies, and food. They even introduced me to a hairdresser who did my hair for free, and in return, I worked at her shop as a shampoo girl from the age of ten all the way through high school. She mentored me and taught me how to apply relaxers, color, weaves, and more.

One of the church leaders was a deacon, and he took a special liking to me, even more than to my sister. One year, it was close to the end of the summer, and he offered to take me shopping for school clothes. Admittedly, I thought it was weird that he only invited me and not my sister, but he explained that another member was going to take her shopping. It felt strange, but I dismissed the feeling because I was so excited not to have to wear clothes from the Salvation Army or thrift stores and be teased (as this was commonplace), so I went with it.

I don't remember which stores we went to, but he was constantly telling me how beautiful I was and how I had a beautiful shape for my age. It made me feel extremely uncomfortable. A little backstory: I have always been very curvy, and I developed at a very young age. From as early as I can remember, it had been commonplace for grown men to flirt with me. His advances were not unusual, to say the least, but because I held my church family in such high regard, it made me feel worse than the other experiences. He would pick out very close-fitting dresses and stand outside of the fitting room asking me to model the dresses for him.

At one point, he came up behind me in the dressing room and placed his body so close that I could feel his penis rub up against my butt. I quickly ran back into the dressing room. Despite my previous sexual experiences, this one felt extremely painful because of the level of trust, admiration, and respect I had for him. It was as if the one place I felt safe had proved that safety was just a myth, and no matter where I went or who I came in contact with, this was my destiny. I remember leaving the fitting room and being quiet for the remainder of the time we were together. I could not wait for him to drop me off at home. I thanked him for taking me shopping because I was still truly grateful, just devastated by the experience.

This was a turning point in my life because, as a result of that experience, my self-esteem was destroyed. Through therapy, I realized that this experience and the one with my uncle made me view myself differently, and as a result, I began to stop caring about my physical appearance. I went through a phase of having bad hygiene, believing that if I didn't look desirable or smell desirable, people would no longer physically abuse me or make sexual advances toward me. (This is one sign of sexual abuse. At the end of the book, I list many more signs of sexual abuse.) This issue haunted me throughout middle school and high school.

There was a lady at the church I was extremely close with. In some instances, I felt closer to her than I did my own family. I told her how he had made me feel uncomfortable, but I begged her not to tell, as I was afraid he would get into trouble at the church. She told me that my responsibility was to feel protected and not to put his comfort above my own. This is something that I struggle with to this day. I often put others' feelings and interests ahead of my own. She assured me that she would speak with him and make sure he knew that it was not acceptable for him to make me feel unsafe in any way. How I felt reminded me of when I had felt responsible for my aunt's divorce: I didn't want to hurt anyone—him, his wife, or his children—and as a result, I immediately regretted speaking up. Despite my desire to shrink back, she kept reassuring me that I didn't do anything wrong.

Several days later, my pastor and the woman, who was a leader at the church, approached me and told me they were sorry this had happened to me and assured me that he would never do anything inappropriate to me again. They later called the deacon into the room, and he apologized for making me feel uncomfortable and, of course, tried to downplay his actions by saying he was just looking at me to make sure the clothes fit properly and not in a sexual way. We both knew the truth, but I so desperately wanted to put that behind me that I accepted his apology and moved on.

While some may downplay some of the instances in this chapter, I know for a fact they changed my perception and view of myself and destroyed my trust in men. I know there are many others who have had even worse experiences and even more violent instances of rape and incest. For me, it's about the negative impact that this type of abuse has on a child, and anyone for that matter. Specifically, it shapes the way children view sex, and just like me, many blame themselves for what happened to them. As I mentioned briefly, the incidents that happened with my cousin (and other similar incidents that happened with her sister), my mother's boyfriend, my uncle, and now the deacon at the church all made me feel an immense sense of blame and shame. I believed it had to be something I was doing wrong to make this continually happen to me. I literally remember feeling like I should wear baggy clothes to hide my body and that if my hygiene wasn't good, people wouldn't want to touch me. This makes me emotional even now writing this book because no child should ever feel that it's their fault that perverted people are viewing them sexually. Furthermore, introducing any type of sexual act, conversation, or action to a child at an early age can have lasting effects on that child.

When talking to women who were victims of sexual assault as children, I learned that these women find themselves either being overly sexual or the opposite, hating the idea of sex and sexuality. This has a lasting effect on people, and often, the thought process continues to haunt them later in life and is magnified when an event or situation occurs that brings that trauma back up to the surface. Even in my own life, despite my years of therapy, healing, and self-acceptance, I still see those fears and triggers being manifest in my relationships. If I am completely honest, I can attribute my toxic and abusive relationships to those incidents. I didn't truly see my value and worth because the sexual abuse made me feel worthless. It made me feel as if all any man would ever see was sex when he looked at me, and that was all I was worth to men. That alone is a harsh reality to come to terms with.

As I end this chapter and introduce some additional information, I want to leave my readers with this thought: everyone's trauma is different, and just because one person's trauma through sexual abuse may be different from another person's, both are equally devastating and will require intentional effort to heal and overcome the wounds that have occurred. In my journey as a youth counselor and now as a life coach, I realize that one thing remains true—people who were sexually assaulted, abused, molested, raped, or fondled all share the same common issue: they are deeply impacted to such a point that it affects their adult lives and often causes them to have poor self-esteem, feelings of being unloved, and feelings of being unworthy. Each one has to make a conscious and intentional effort to heal from the trauma that has occurred. The sad truth is that, even with healing, there will always be some residual effects of sexual assault, and victims must make a conscious effort not to let that trauma overtake and overshadow their happiness.

If I could wish for one thing, it would be that all victims of sexual abuse and assault could heal and know that the incidents that happened to them don't have to define their future, success, and ability to find love, protection, and security. Sharing my own personal story is difficult, but every time I want to quit or keep quiet about my story, there is a fire burning inside of me that lets me know that I am serving a higher purpose, helping others get to that place of healing. Anyone who knows me personally knows that I am private about my personal life, but after my experiences with sexual assault in my own life and learning what happened with other family members close to me, I knew I had to break my silence. If I remained silent and kept it a secret, the abuse would continue to be a generational curse, and I knew I had a duty and responsibility to ensure that the curse over my family and over generations to come was broken.

— CHAPTER 4 —

To Move Forward, Sometimes You Have to Take a Step Back

The next few chapters are going to be even more difficult to write because the stories don't just involve me. I always view myself as strong and don't mind when I have to go through tough things, as much as it bothers me to know that others are hurting. Dealing with this trauma and rehashing the past is something I am doing for the greater good. However, I am not comfortable going back to the pasts of family members. But this is necessary in order for those who are reading to understand how/why this is a generational curse. This will give a clear picture of why I felt compelled to take certain steps to protect my children, which I will share in later chapters.

I will be very cautious not to give too many intimate details about the events of others, as I believe their story is for them to share, but I want my readers and listeners to know that this journey started generations before me, and I am absolutely convinced that the reason it continued in my generation is because of the secrets that were kept hidden and the lies that were told that protected the pedophiles in our family and ultimately forced the victims, innocent children, to carry the lies and secrets for years.

While my details will not mention names, I am compelled to dispel the shame, lies, and secrets that opened the door for abuse to continue, even affecting my children.

While I can't speak to the sexual abuse that happened before my mother, I can share what I learned over the course of my journey and mission to break the generational curse over our family. She has given me express permission to share her story because she knows that healing will take place for our family as well as for any other families who come into contact with this book. Sharing this will also hopefully help others heal and take a stand against sexual assault and incest. I have truly begun to accept that discussing these topics will help to free so many people and allow them to boldly stand up and break the curses for themselves.

Before I begin to speak on my mom's story, I would like the reader to know that she is one of the kindest, sweetest, most loving, caring, and forgiving people I know. She is my biggest inspiration because of the grace and love that she shows to everyone she comes into contact with. She has been victimized so many times in her life that I can't even count, but it never stopped her from being an amazing and loving person. My actual knowledge of her trauma is limited because she is very discreet, but with the knowledge I do have, she has been through more in her life than most people ever experience.

My mother's initial instances of trauma through sexual abuse began at a very young age, from six years of age through nine years of age. Her young, tender age is devastating enough to have had such a terrible experience, but even more terrible was the fact that her abuser was her own father. Let me preface this situation by saying that her father was a severe alcoholic at this time, and I am now coming to the knowledge that he, too, was sexually abused. While that fact in no way justifies or excuses his actions, I merely mention this because it goes to show that this generational curse dates back several generations.

According to my mother, the sexual abuse started as fondling and elevated to him slowly introducing sodomy. I asked if her mother ever had any knowledge of this or even suspected anything. She explained that her mom was often passed out drunk when these incidents would occur. Similar to my childhood, my mom and her siblings grew up in a house where there were a lot of neighborhood friends and people in and out of the home. Both of my grandparents were severe alcoholics and would often have very nasty drunk friends over who would say nasty and inappropriate comments to the children, and I'm pretty sure they would even try to touch them if my grandparents were passed out drunk.

My mom did not disclose any details of her first time being fondled but admitted that the fondling slowly progressed to actual anal penetration. When she shared this with me, it made me sick and caused me to burst into tears. I never knew any of this information until a few years ago. Out of all of my mother's children, I was the closest to my grandfather. I adored him despite his alcohol addiction. I actually relocated to assist her with caring for him before he passed away and to help take care of her, so *devastated* isn't even a strong enough word to describe how I felt after learning this. She went on to explain that he told her he would never "take her virginity," and this is the reason he chose to penetrate her anally. It makes me emotional just thinking of this happening to a child and, even worse, a child that young. She also said that he would sometimes penetrate her too deeply, and it would cause her to bleed and have small tears in her anus. This abuse continued for three years. Once she was close to reaching the age of puberty, he stopped because I guess he didn't want to impregnate her by mistake.

I had to ask her how she was able to keep this secret for so many years from her mother and siblings. She explained that right before he stopped doing this to her, he broke down in tears and explained to her that he, too, had been assaulted (though he never gave any details) and had never meant to do this to her but felt as though the demons in him had caused him to do it. This was the first time he had told anyone this secret that he had buried for years, and I assume that because my mother was his first victim, in some way this made him vulnerable enough at the moment to voice his own challenges with sexual assault. He further explained how he was a terrible human and that he no longer wanted to live because he was afraid he would hurt someone else. While I don't doubt that he felt sympathy or even that he was battling with a demonic force bigger than himself, I believe he manipulated my mother in some way to make her not feel safe enough to tell. While I can't prove it, I believe that she was also abused by some of his drunk friends or other family members because, when he lived with us and we were younger, some of his friends used to be inappropriate with us, though there are still gaps in my childhood that I blocked out, and I honestly can't remember despite my many years in therapy.

I wish that the stories of abuse ended there, but, unfortunately, her story gets even worse. My mother never told me when the abuse started with her next perpetrator: my great-uncle. He was some years older than her, and he took the abuse to the next level, which affected my mom for the rest of her life. Based on the conversation I had with my mother, my great-uncle was always looking at her inappropriately and being inappropriate with her. This did not surprise me because he always seemed creepy to me and my siblings. There was a time period where we lived with my great-grandmother, and he lived there with her too. He always gave everyone the creeps when he was around, not just from a perverted standpoint, but also because he was this egotistical person who had a literal god complex. He would talk about how he was god and that everyone should worship him. He would even go so far as to say he was from some made-up planet. Needless to say, we all knew he wasn't wrapped too tight.

My mother said that he would often come over and drink with my grandfather and his friends, and when everyone was passed out drunk, he would lurk around in her bedroom with her and her sisters. She said that he, too, began molesting her and sodomizing her initially. And he kept doing it for years because he knew that she was so timid and would never tell. It progressed, and he became bolder and began to sodomize her more, eventually ejaculating in her, and she became pregnant at the age of fourteen. She hid her pregnancy from her mother, father, and siblings as long as she could. She felt so ashamed and embarrassed that she would not tell who had impregnated her. She lied to her mother and told her that it was a stranger who had raped her.

While this alone is devastating and heartbreaking, it gets worse: no one believed her. Her mother took her to the doctor, and because her hymen was still intact, the doctor assumed that she'd had consensual sex with someone—maybe a boyfriend. He suggested to her parents that he (the possible boyfriend) had ejaculated on her and the sperm had impregnated her because of the fact that her hymen was not broken. Her mother believed that she was lying about being raped. I can't even imagine the mental anguish my mother experienced having to live with this secret and then being accused of lying when she had actually been assaulted by a family member who was able to continue to come into the home and abuse her over and over again. Her story is so hard to even write because, even now, it makes me want to just grab her and protect her from everything and everyone who has ever hurt her.

Despite the shame and verbal abuse she sustained by being called a liar, my mother chose to have the baby. She became a mother to my sister when she was only fifteen years old. This is hard to even speak of. She told me that her delivery was the most torture anyone could imagine enduring because she had to deliver my sister while she was physically a virgin. My brain can't even comprehend the pain and anguish this caused her, but she decided that, despite how she had become pregnant, she still wanted to give my sister a chance at life. What an amazingly strong woman she is, and it often makes me think of all the women who, despite being raped, still choose to birth children. There is no greater sacrifice and higher love that I could imagine. I always said that if it were me, I would have gotten an abortion. The fact is that every time I would look at my child, I would have to relive that trauma. That would be more than I could bear. Beyond that fact, giving birth to a baby whose father was my uncle would add even more layers of trauma and pain.

Before I continue, I want to explain that she was not only ridiculed by family members who actually judged her and called her a slut, she was also treated terribly by the doctor who cared for her during her pregnancy and was judged and ridiculed for years. This is one of the reasons that, to this day, I am super protective over my mother and would die and kill for her. She never had the protection of anyone, not even her father, who is supposed to be the person who keeps you safe from people who would seek to cause you harm. Instead of protecting her, he continued this vicious cycle of abuse that damaged her in ways that are too painful to speak on.

I have to mention that my mom never told my sister who her father was. This is something that was revealed to me out of the blue many years later. We were all told that my mother was raped by a stranger when she was younger, and no one had ever known who he was or how to find him. I want you all to sit back and imagine the amount of pressure and turmoil it caused her to live with that lie, to share it with her siblings and parents, and to also be ridiculed and judged by the family for being a teen mother. It makes my blood boil just thinking about it. Even after I found out the truth, I never blamed or judged my mother: it would've been easier to deal with had it been a stranger. I know this was probably the only way she could mentally cope with the pain.

It's interesting now that I think back to my childhood—we always noticed that my sister shared some of the same mannerisms as my great-uncle and even laughed like him. As children, we would laugh and joke about how we thought he was her father because of the similar mannerisms and personality traits. Don't get me wrong. My sister is amazing, and she is extremely intelligent, like he was, and has some of his same characteristics—fortunately, only the good ones. Additionally, my sister struggled because she felt this sense of anger toward her father as well as wanting to know who he was. I again can't imagine what that felt like when she was very young. Fortunately, my mother's brothers lived with us for many of our formative years, and they were at least some male figures in her life.

Once I found out the truth of what had happened with my great-uncle and grandfather, it made me extremely angry that we were around both of them all the time growing up and even lived with my grandfather and great-uncle for periods of time. I cannot say for certain that neither of them touched me growing up because there are still years of my childhood that are missing from my memory, which is most likely for the best. Additionally, with my grandfather's alcoholic friends in and out of the house all the time, we never really felt safe. We, however, were smart enough to always stay together so that none of us were ever alone with them.

I want everyone to bear in mind that I did not learn of these incidents until a few years ago when I had the opportunity to break this curse. The way I found out that my great-uncle was my sister's father was through a supernatural experience that I will discuss later. I literally learned of this incident years before I even understood *why* the Spirit of God revealed it to me. I will also mention that the details regarding my grandfather did not come out until after he was already deceased. Despite the fact that the sexual abuse happened between my grandfather and my mom, I felt a sense of betrayal because my grandfather was the only consistent father figure in my life. While his alcoholism caused him to be less than he could be, he still loved me and always made me feel special and valued. I felt betrayed because I am sure that if I had known of these issues/incidents, I would've hated him. Because my mother is the sweet person that she is, she never wanted us to look at him differently. I also now know, after years of therapy, that her actions were a result of Stockholm syndrome, which the Cleveland Clinic defines as a coping mechanism to being held captive where victims "form a psychological connection with their captors and begin sympathizing with them." While I have never professed to be a certified therapist, I am a life coach and a person who studied psychology in college, and I definitely recognize those traits in her. I am in no way blaming or belittling her, just explaining why some of the actions and steps she took after I told her my instances of abuse would've been different if she had been in a healthier mental state.

Additionally, my purpose in writing this book is to help people heal, recognize the generational curse of incest, and provide people with the strength to ensure justice is served. In later chapters, I will discuss how I stepped up and did something that had not been done before in my family: I made an abuser pay for his actions. My ultimate goal is to eliminate the shame surrounding incest, rape, molestation, and sexual assault and to bring to more victims the strength to speak up and hold abusers accountable for their actions.

— CHAPTER 5 —

How My Past Sexual Abuse Caused Me to Choose Wrong

In the last chapter, I mentioned how it was necessary to start from the (possible) beginning of the generational curse of incest and molestation. In this chapter, I want to go back through my journey to discuss how sexual abuse caused me to have low self-esteem, which resulted in me staying in toxic relationships. I believe that had my self-esteem been better, I would have removed myself from those toxic relationships much sooner. I also want to remind you that, in a previous chapter, I mentioned that I had bad hygiene on purpose growing up, trying to make myself less attractive so that men would stop looking at me sexually. This truth came to me after years of therapy and healing and became more clear while writing this book.

While I spent time in church learning how to cope with the pain of my experiences and even having therapy occasionally, I still carried some of the weight and results of that trauma with me. As a child, my father was not involved in my life. The main reason for this was because he was extremely physically and verbally abusive to my mother. Thankfully, she was eventually strong enough to get away from him and protect us from him.

My few memories of my father are not good ones. My first memory is of him coming in the house while my mom, my siblings, and I were in the kitchen helping her tenderize liver. He barged into the kitchen, snatched the knife out of her hand, and put it up against her neck for absolutely no reason. In addition to this drunken incident, I remember him coming to our church when we were younger and causing a scene, again because of his drunkenness. To add insult to injury, he has not ever spoken more than a few words to me in my life. He used to talk to my sister, clearly showing an affinity to her, but not me or my twin brother. The few times that I recall seeing him triggered anger in me as I reflected on what he did to my mother. He was a sheer embarrassment to me. I honestly never desired a relationship with him and never felt the need for him in my life. My grandfather was a severe alcoholic at one point, but then he cleaned his life up and became a better person. As a result, he was the only father figure I knew, which made me never regret not having my father around.

Despite having my grandfather as a father figure, I realize as a healed version of myself that my first experiences of sexual assault and abuse resulted in me not really seeing my value, and I realize I was never protected in my childhood. I was left vulnerable and susceptible to negative relationships. The lack of fatherly direction led to a tendency to be drawn to the wrong type of man. Though my grandfather was present as a father figure after overcoming alcoholism, there was still a lack of guidance that should've come from a father.

My first husband and I were married fresh out of high school. I liked him because he seemed to like me beyond my physical appearance. He was funny, and, despite having two children with another woman at such a young age, I didn't judge him. I thought our relationship was good. Looking back at this situation as an adult, I now realize there were several red flags that I would've seen had I had a positive self-concept and the guidance of a father. One red flag that I should've noticed was how verbally abusive he was to his children's mother, his mother, and his grandmother. This should've been a clear sign of how he would treat me.

Nevertheless, we ended up getting married after he completed boot camp while I was a freshman in college. We then relocated to another state and lived in a military community. For the first two years of our marriage, we were very much in love with one another. We were connected with a really great church, and, despite all of the naysayers, we were happy and had a successful marriage. It wasn't until we relocated to Atlanta and had our first child together that he began to show his true abusive colors. When he got stationed in Atlanta, we were excited because we used to go at least twice a month to visit this church that we watched on television and had fallen in love with.

The first year in Atlanta was good, but I noticed a change in him after we purchased our home and he began to work a second job. He was very adamant about me staying at home with our daughter, so I did. I noticed that he stopped calling on his breaks, and, eventually, that led to him staying out late at night and sometimes never even coming home. I knew in my gut that something was wrong, but when I would confront him, his temper would flare up out of control, and he would eventually fight me physically.

Now, I have to pause here quickly because watching my mother go through domestic abuse in several of her relationships made me refuse to sit there and take physical or verbal abuse from a man. I am definitely a fighter and would always go toe to toe with him.

Eventually, the lies and deception stopped, and he became blatant with his cheating, drinking, and abuse. I can vividly recall a day I was checking all the pockets of our clothes before loading them into the laundry, and I found a list of at least ten names of different women along with their physical descriptions (e.g., Linda with the big butt) and their phone numbers. When I confronted him with this information, he got defensive, of course, and tried to deflect. This led to a physical fight between us where he choked me to the point of almost passing out, and I sliced his arm with one of the ceramic figures we had made in pottery class.

This was the beginning of five years of turbulence between us before we finally decided to divorce. Ironically, he married one of the women he had cheated on me with ten days later. I only mention this part of my story to say that the emotional and mental toll that past episodes of sexual abuse and witnessing physical abuse had on me caused me to choose the wrong type of men. Looking back at my first marriage, as well as the second, I noticed that my brokenness caused me to draw broken people to me. As a result, I suffered more trials, drama, and tribulation than I ever should have. However, I will be the first to admit that my trials caused me to be the woman that I am today, and I literally don't have one regret for my journey.

Unfortunately, my first marriage didn't teach me all of the healing lessons I needed to learn, but my second one definitely taught me those additional lessons. I admit that my second marriage was a total rebound from my first husband. I was still very young, and since I didn't have much real relationship experience to begin with, I fell into this trap again. My second husband was not even someone I was physically attracted to or someone I wanted to have a relationship with initially. I knew he was interested in me, but because I was still healing from my divorce, I wasn't in the mental space for a relationship. He came in as a friend and a support system through the emotional turmoil that I went through during my divorce. As time went on, he wore my guard down through the kindness and support he showed me. This, of course, was short-lived. Shortly after I decided to date him, I saw signs of a bad temper and a lack of accountability when it came to how he handled his children. Still oblivious, I decided to continue the relationship with him.

He showed his true colors a few days after we were married, which was the first time he hit me. I'll never forget it! We were driving in my car, and we had a small disagreement about something. The next thing I knew, he slapped me with an open hand while I was driving, causing me to swerve off the road. I was in total shock. It wasn't like we were having a major argument or fight; it was really something minor. I remember thinking, *I just married him, so maybe it isn't too late to get the marriage annulled.*

I was literally so mentally exhausted after battling for five years with my ex-husband and trying to save that marriage that I just didn't have the emotional or physical strength to fight again. One of the leaders at the church we were going to at the time came by the house and spoke with us. I remember he reprimanded him for putting his hands on me, and he told us that the only way the marriage would work was if we made a point to never say things to one another that would trigger one another and cause the other to lash out.

This is a philosophy I still believe to be true. What this lesson taught me over the course of time was that despite his anger issues, I had to analyze why I had accepted this behavior, not only from him, but also from my first husband. When I think back to how angry I was when I witnessed my father mentally destroy and physically abuse my mother, and how my instances of sexual abuse made me indignant to such a point I would get protective over everyone I loved, it finally dawned on me that I saw everyone as worthy of being protected but myself. It was as if everyone else was worthy of being saved from trauma except for me. I truly believe that this warped mentality was the reason I was even able to get myself connected with these types of individuals. My lack of understanding in self-love and accepting these as normal behaviors in relationships caused me to make terrible decisions that affected me most of my life. It wasn't until my mid-thirties that I truly discovered who I was and what I deserved and finally mustered up the strength to demand better for myself. While some of my healing took place during my time in the Praying Wives Ministry, I still had considerable knowledge to gain and learning to do about myself, what was normal and acceptable behavior in relationships, and how to stand up for what I deserved.

Another fact that dawned on me after years of healing was that my lack of a positive father figure and being violated by men I respected and trusted in my life left me open and vulnerable to bad relationships. I don't regret any of the paths that my life has taken. While this may sound strange to some, I have learned over the years on my healing journey that all of my experiences played a role in shaping me into the woman I am today, and as a result, I have no regrets.

In the next few chapters, I will be discussing how I broke the generational curse of incest and molestation over my family. These next few chapters will help bring all of those experiences together and reveal how they brought me to the place in my life where I no longer allowed myself to be a victim, but be victorious.

— CHAPTER 6 —

How the Past Was Revealed and Would be Useful in My Future

I want to start this chapter by going back a few years prior to the instances that occurred with the next generation. It was the morning after my graduation from getting my master's degrees. My best friend and two of my sisters had come to town to celebrate with me. After a long night of celebrating, we all curled up in my king-size bed. This was nothing new for us, coming from such a large family; we often had to sleep in the same bed.

I'll never forget this: I was suddenly awakened out of my sleep by the audible voice of God. Now, I know this may sound weird to some, and not surprising to others. There have only been four times in my entire life where I actually heard the audible voice of God speaking to me. The first time was when I was just ten years old, and I was at church sitting in the choir stand. I heard the audible voice tell me as clear as a person standing next to me that the pastor was going to call me up to pray during the service. Within minutes of hearing that voice, my pastor called me up to pray. While this may not seem like a big deal to many, from my experiences, it's something you will never forget when it happens to you, and it will change your perspective forever on how real God is and how he loves us so deeply that he takes the time to speak to us individually.

Back to the incident that occurred when I was lying in bed next to my best friend and sisters. I literally heard the audible voice of God tell me that my great-uncle was my sister's father. It made me sit straight up in the bed and look over at my sister and weep. While I'd never had proof of this reality until that very moment, my other siblings and I had always suspected that this was the case because of the similarities in their mannerisms. So to fast-forward years later and have our intuition confirmed was almost too difficult to comprehend.

A few moments after I sat up in bed, my best friend woke up and asked me what was wrong. I told her what I had just heard. She looked at me and asked me what I was going to do. I told her that I felt obligated to tell my sister what I'd just learned. However, I didn't understand why God had shared this with me and not with my sister, who this actually affected. I definitely didn't understand the significance of the information shared, nor did I know why he shared it with me, until years later.

When my sister finally woke up, I told her what was shared with me, and she immediately dismissed it. She told me things she'd learned about my mom and how people in the family suspected that my grandfather had sexually abused my mother—and they suspected that he could potentially be her father. I was shocked because I had not known about the sexual abuse that my mom experienced by her father or her uncle prior to this incident.

My sister said that she even suspected another uncle of potentially being her father. After this incident, I didn't mention it again for a few years until one day I was speaking with one of my aunts, and as we were speaking about generational curses, the topic came up. I told her about hearing the audible voice of God waking me from my sleep and the information that I heard. She gasped, paused, and said to me, "How did you know?" I asked her how *she* knew about this prior to me sharing the information. She told me of an incident when she was younger where she had gotten up in the middle of the night and had seen my great-uncle standing over my mother with a bunch of white stuff on him. She had pretended to sleep and had noticed that my mother was distraught after the incident. She also mentioned that she had never spoken to my mother, or anyone else, about the incident. She had been very young when she'd seen this and probably feared no one would believe her. She further explained that she did not want to bring up the incident to my mother because she didn't want to cause her any additional shame, pain, or embarrassment.

Unaware of how this information would be useful to me in the future, I went on with life, but I never let the information leave my mind. I hesitated to confront my mother about whether or not the incidents were true so as not to cause her to relive the pain. I also felt that it wasn't really my place to ask or question her, as that should have been reserved for my sister, who was most affected by this. I backed off from mentioning anything about it for years because I felt that my mother had been through so much trauma, and knowing her personality, having to relive these moments would hurt her.

The moment that the Spirit of God shared that information became the turning point for some really major things in my life. I can literally go back in my mind and see how my entire life changed. I began to focus more on healing from my past trauma and take a firm stand on protecting my mental health. I began therapy for myself and my children to help them cope with the divorces. I wanted to get to a place of healing, not just for myself, but for my entire family.

Shortly after this incident, my children and I relocated back to my hometown. I needed a fresh start after my divorce. Additionally, my grandfather was very ill, and my mom had recently been diagnosed with an autoimmune disease. She moved my grandfather in with her, and she was taking care of him while trying to manage the autoimmune disease. I knew that it was the best time for me to get more time with my grandfather, whom I adored and had a close bond with, as mentioned in previous chapters. He was the only father figure I had, and after he had stopped drinking, he had become a much better person.

It was not an easy transition to leave the only home the children had ever known, but I knew that healing needed to happen for myself as well as my children. When we relocated, I moved in with my mom, whose house was already overpopulated with my grandfather, three of my brothers, my mom's boyfriend, and now me and my two young children. As we are from a very large family anyway, we were pretty accustomed to sharing small spaces. I left the place where I had lived for nearly twenty years and made that transition to my hometown despite how much I didn't like the area that I grew up in because of crime. Not to mention that my children had grown accustomed to living in the suburbs of Atlanta, and I had deliberately protected them from living in bad neighborhoods and had worked hard to provide a certain life for them. I knew that the time spent in the ghetto was going to be short-lived for me and my children. However, my focus was on assisting my mother with taking care of my grandfather, so I knew once I got there, I had to hit the ground running, finding employment and establishing a fresh start for myself.

When I first got to my hometown, I started driving for Uber and Lyft, working a full-time job as an HR manager, and also working part-time at a medical lab as a lab tech. I hustled hard to get my finances in order and to move out of my mother's place. I remember stepping out in faith and applying for apartments. There was one I applied for that was close to my jobs and was upscale. It would allow me to get the kids in a good school district and start the life that I wanted for my family.

After several months of saving, paying off debt, and getting approved for my new apartment, I was able to build the life I wanted for myself and my children. After we moved, the children enjoyed being in our new place and started making new friends at their new school. It was a happy and welcome change, especially since my mom's house was overcrowded and the crime in her area was very bad. I knew that this was more of the level that my kids and I were used to prior to moving back home.

I continued working extremely hard in order to pay the rent and bills in this new place, but it didn't bother me because it was worth it. Because my work schedule was so busy and the kids were younger, I would often have one of my younger brothers watch them for me. It was a welcome change for him as well because he was out of work. In fact, when my kids and I had moved into the basement of my mom's house, he had lived on the other side of the basement, so the kids were comfortable with him, and he needed a break from such a busy household as well.

He initially came over only periodically, but as I began to work more, he would come over more frequently to get away but also to help take care of the kids while I was working both jobs and still driving for Uber and Lyft. My mom's house did not have internet, so he was able to use my internet and extra computer to apply for jobs, and I was helping him craft his resume so that he could find work. It was challenging for him because he didn't have a car, and my new apartment was not on a bus or train line, so he had to be driven where he needed to go. Eventually, I was able to help him with his resume and to get a job at a security company. It was on a bus line, so he was then able to get to and from his job, and I could pick him up from the train station or drop him off after I finished my jobs.

At this time, the support that he offered was priceless because I was finally able to get some help with the kids while doing what I needed to do to ensure we had more than enough money to pay the bills and to ensure that my kids could live as comfortably as possible. I was not getting any type of consistent support from my ex-husband, which was in no way a shock, so having multiple jobs was the only option I had to take care of my family and responsibilities.

Eventually, my brother began to stay weeks at a time. This made me feel like my life was finally coming together, having the support I needed for my kids while taking care of my responsibilities as the sole provider for my family.

After nearly two years of working like a complete dog, I was laid off from my part-time job at the lab. This was a big blow for me financially, and I knew that I would be unable to maintain the bills at my current place, so once again, I would have to make some financial adjustments. Unfortunately, despite my position at my main job, it did not pay nearly enough to afford the rent in the luxury apartment. The only option was to go back to stay with my mom in order to get back on my feet financially and possibly save enough money to afford to live on my own again comfortably.

I was devastated because, yet again, I had to take several steps backward and uproot my children. The living arrangement was a blessing, but I had finally gotten my kids to the place where they were stable, especially after the divorce and relocating. Despite having to disappoint my kids again by moving away from the home they absolutely adored, I knew that I could not uproot them from their school, the martial arts classes, and, most importantly, their friends. So I decided that, despite the drive, I would use a friend's address to keep them in their school and after-school activities. This would maintain at least some level of consistency and normalcy in their lives. And that's exactly what I did.

Fortunately, the move was not too much of a disappointment for the kids because, after all, they were with their favorite uncle and their grandmother. During this time, my children and I were very fortunate to get a few more months with my grandfather, who was getting progressively more ill. It also worked out for me because I could help my mother care for my grandfather, and I was able to still take care of my responsibility of working to earn more money. Our living arrangement was the same: we slept in the basement on one side while my brother resided on the other side. The basement was fairly large, as it spanned the entire length of the house, so we had enough space for all of us to sleep comfortably despite how overcrowded the house was in general.

When we made the transition, it was hectic, of course, having to compensate for the drive and the extra gas, but I was really focused on getting my finances in order and building my business. This was when I first started focusing on my HR consulting business, and I was busy applying for my federal and state certifications. It was a time in my life when I was definitely in business-building mode and had mentally shifted from working hard for other people to working for myself. I was still holding down my main job and no longer working my part-time job, but I was still doing Uber and Lyft part-time. Able to release much of my financial burden, I could really hone in on building my business and focus my energy on building a solid, financially secure future for myself and my children. As a single mom, who, at best, had very off-and-on child support from my ex-husband, I needed to find a way to get financially secure without having to depend on any support from him. Living with my mom afforded me the opportunity to take care of all of my responsibilities as far as saving and building a business, and it also provided me with the support I needed with the kids while I worked to build a better life for us as a family.

During this time, I was also there to make sure my mom was taking care of her health condition, and it gave me some much-needed time to get closer to her after being away for so long. When my grandfather passed away, my mother no longer received the financial support that she had gotten from his check, so I was able to help by paying a portion of her rent. I'm sure this financial help was needed at the time. We were all living in a place of contentment, but it was short-lived.

This particular year, I was invited to go to Hawaii with my best friend, who was working there for a period of time conducting training. Because she already had a room booked there, I was more than happy to just book a flight and spend a few days with her. I needed this vacation more than I knew; I didn't realize how hard I had been working, burning the candle at both ends, if you will, to the point where I had lost sight of being balanced enough to relax and have fun.

Needless to say, when the offer came to travel (which is one of my favorite things to do), I was more than ready to jump on this opportunity. I booked my flight and arrived in Hawaii, and I remember checking in with my mother to make sure that my children were good.

She assured me everything was fine, and I booked a rental car so that I could get around while my friend was working.

A little backstory on me: I am a very adventurous person who loves to see the world. I packed my journal so that I could write and plan for my business ventures as well as spend some time getting closer to God. I had been seeking his direction concerning my business, and I wanted to heal from a break-up with a guy I'd started dating when I'd relocated. I knew that this trip would be just the getaway that I needed to bring peace and clarity to my life. I looked forward to exploring Hawaii alone during the day and hanging out with my friend and her coworkers at night. After an amazing couple of days in Hawaii, I returned home and was told that my daughter was acting a little weird and standoffish. I didn't think much of it at that time because, when I asked her about it, she said she was okay. I let it go, and things went back to normal. Little did I know that this event would be quite significant in the next few months.

― CHAPTER 7 ―

The Most Painful Part of This Journey

I was awakened one night to a rustling noise in the corner of my room. Initially, I thought the sound was maybe a mouse that had come through the window, which was highly likely in the basement and the neighborhood where we were living. I looked up and didn't see anything, so I laid my head back down. A few minutes later, I heard the sound again. This time, I sat up in my bed, which was located directly next to my daughters' bed. I turned the cell phone light on and was startled and shocked to witness my brother jumping up out of the bed next to my daughter. When I asked what he was doing, he attempted to lie to me and tell me that he had gotten out of his bed, which was on the opposite side of the basement, to investigate a noise. Immediately, I called him out on that lie and said to him, "Even if you heard what you thought was a mouse, why are you getting up from the girls' bed?" He tried to convince me that this was the reason he was in the corner and in her bed. After hearing me speaking to him, my girls woke up. I immediately told them to get up and go to the bathroom.

I feel the need to explain what I did next: as a person who was molested in the past, I knew that child molesters and rapists often sodomize their victims in order to make sure that they don't break a girl's hymen. I had experienced this myself and also knew that my mother had been molested in this same sick way, so I knew to look out for signs and/or evidence of sodomy and to see if her hymen was broken.

People may wonder how I remained calm and clearheaded. I am always super calm under pressure, not because of my own strength, but because I'm such an action-oriented person, I immediately step into action. My emotions tend to kick in afterward. That was exactly what happened this time. I went upstairs to the bathroom with my daughters and asked the one he'd been closest to if my brother had touched her inappropriately or put his penis inside of her or on her at any point. She denied it and looked terrified. She said, "I was asleep, and I don't know what he was doing." I checked her anatomy and her underwear to see if there was any evidence of semen or trauma in her private areas.

Afterward, I told her to get dressed, and we immediately went to look for a plastic bag to place all of her clothing and underwear in so that I could preserve any evidence. The entire time I was in action mode, my brother was following me upstairs and pleading his case, telling lies about how he was only in her bed trying to see if there was a mouse in the corner. By this point, most of my family members in the house were awake. I was so focused on preserving the evidence that none of the external things going on around me even occurred to me until afterward. I told the kids to get dressed so that we could all leave together.

Meanwhile, my brother was still pleading his case and saying that I misunderstood what I had witnessed with my own eyes. My emotions hadn't kicked in at this point. I'm grateful that they hadn't because I probably would've done something that I would have regretted and wouldn't have been able to take back. When I recount the events that transpired, I'm shocked myself because I know that I could've blacked out and taken his life at that point. I'm still in awe of the grace of God that was obviously over and on me because PTSD is a real thing, Honestly, I always said that if someone ever tried to rape, molest, or harm any of my kids in any way, I would kill them with no hesitation. We don't know the strength we have until we're faced with the situation.

At this point, it was almost time for the kids to go to school, but I knew, despite the fact that they had a test that day, I needed to take care of this situation to ensure that they were safe. My mom heard the commotion and came downstairs to the living room where the kids and I were getting our coats and shoes on to go to the police station.

She asked me what happened, and I explained that I had caught my brother jumping out of my daughters' bed and how he denied it despite me seeing it with my own eyes. She, of course, wanted to talk to him and said that she would see what happened from him. While I don't fault my mother, I know that she suffers from Stockholm syndrome, so I didn't expect her response to be anything other than what it was. I told her that I didn't have anything to talk about because I knew what I saw, and, more importantly, I was not going to stand around and pretend that it didn't happen. I knew I had a responsibility to my child first and foremost to protect her. Secondly, I could not allow this cycle of protecting abusers by keeping secrets of molestation, thereby keeping the victims silenced and forced to keep their violations a secret, to continue. As I mentioned in earlier chapters, I understand now why my mother, and even my aunts, did not act when I thought something should have been done about my abusers. It was taught for generations, not just in my family, but in many, many others, to keep this type of thing a secret.

I placed the kids in the car and proceeded to drive to the police station that was near my mom's house. I entered the police station alone while the kids were in the car. When I arrived, I asked to speak to an officer who could give me some guidance on how to report the incident that I saw. I explained the events that occurred, and after the officer listened to my account of the events, he asked me to sit in the waiting area. A different officer greeted me and told me that this particular precinct did not handle this type of situation. Because of the nature of the charge, I would have to report it to the main precinct downtown. He gave me the name and contact number of the special victims unit (SVU) and told me that an officer would be waiting for me. I then proceeded to the main precinct to meet up with the officer from the special victims unit.

When we arrived at the precinct, I gave the lady at the front desk the name of the officer I was supposed to see and filled out some paperwork. That moment was the first time it began to sink in what had really happened and how devastated I was. I felt a sense of guilt and responsibility for putting my children in this situation. The guilt really began to sink in as I realized how long I had purposely protected my children from pedophiles, going so far as to not allow them to attend sleepovers. It was unimaginably difficult for me to face the fact that I had let my guard down and had allowed my children to be with a monster. The guilt continued to build as I realized that I had let a pedophile into my home and had even helped him find work and get on his feet. Thinking that I was doing a good deed for my family, yet again, had turned into a source of pain and trauma for myself and my family.

While trying to deal with the overwhelming guilt, the detective from the SVU came to speak with me and said that our first stop would be the hospital to get my daughter checked out. He further explained that he would have a representative from child services meet us at the hospital, and she would have to interview her. For a moment, I thought that what she would have to deal with would be almost as devastating as what she had experienced. I feared I was making a mistake making her relive this entire experience.

The officer took my statement, and we headed to the hospital to have her examined.

This was one of the most difficult parts of this journey. I had to explain to her that two doctors and a nurse were going to examine her private parts and take pictures. I also had to explain that she would be interviewed and asked questions by other people (the case workers), and I told her to make sure she told them everything and left nothing out. I reassured her that it was safe for her to tell the truth, that she did nothing wrong, and that telling the truth would help us make sure he was not ever going to hurt her again.

The dreaded moment happened when the doctors, the case worker, and the nurse came into the room. They asked her to disrobe and get into a hospital gown. I remember holding her hand and seeing the look of sheer terror on her face. Despite being scared, she knew I was right there with her, holding her hand and telling her it was okay. I was amazed at how brave she was. She didn't shed a single tear in that moment. I held her hand as they examined her and took samples from her vagina and anus. While the doctor and nurse examined her and took samples, another doctor took pictures. This was my worst nightmare, watching my child go through a real-life episode of *Law & Order: SVU*. I had to be strong for my daughter—she wasn't crying, so I couldn't dare cry, despite the anger, pain, guilt, shame, resentment, and episodes of PTSD that haunted me. I just held her hand and kissed her forehead, reassuring her and telling her how brave she was. That moment will be forever etched in my mind as one of the worst days of my life. I would've much rather it had been me who was brutally raped than for someone to do anything like this to my sweet, innocent child.

I had a myriad of emotions rushing in at once. I was instantly triggered to remember my experience with my uncle and my other instances of trauma from my own childhood. Even more ironic was that the brother who had done this to my daughter was the son of my mother's boyfriend, the same man who used to steal our underwear and watch us take baths through peepholes that he created in the bathroom door. The thing that hurt worse for me was that this brother and I had had several conversations about what his dad did to me and my sisters. To think that he was now doing even worse things to his niece was overwhelming to me.

It was also crystal clear to me why God had shared with me the information about my great-uncle being my sister's father. I hadn't understood why I was the one God had chosen to share that information with until that very moment. It was clear to me that this was a generational curse, and he knew that I, unlike those who had known of it before me, was not going to stand around and allow this cycle of abuse and injustice to continue.

After her initial exam, the detective drove us to the rape crisis center for children, and the case worker followed us there. He told us that he would follow the proper protocol and keep me posted on the results of the case. He reassured me that we were being very brave and that most people don't go through this process because of how hard it is on the victim. He stated that victims oftentimes quit before going all the way through with it. He also told me that if nothing else, my daughter would know how much love I had for her.

At the center, we were greeted by two workers along with the case worker. They sat my daughter in a room with toys, drawing materials, and video games and told her to play while they spoke with me. I was taken into another room and asked to recount the events that I had witnessed. I explained in detail what had occurred, and after conducting the interview with me, they told me they would be interviewing her. It was a total of three women in the room, and they said that once the interview was completed, I would be with her again.

It seemed like my other daughter and I waited forever while she was being interviewed and recorded yet again. It was the most helpless I had felt throughout this entire process. There was nothing I could do to console her or comfort her. I had to trust that she would be comfortable enough to be open and honest with the case workers and tell them the details that needed to be told. I hoped that she would be more open with them than she had been with me. I feared that my brother had threatened her, as my uncle had with me, and/or had even intimidated her so she wouldn't share any details. I remember praying and pleading with God for her to tell the whole truth so that he couldn't do this to anyone else. I prayed that she would be strong and bold and tell the truth without being afraid of possible consequences.

The interview finally ended after what seemed like an eternity. She came out of the room, and the case workers asked to speak to me again. While they couldn't share many details, they did tell me that this was not the first time he had touched her inappropriately. What I was told next took my breath away. While they couldn't go into detail, they said that my brother had been molesting her for a few years, ever since we had relocated. She told them that he had exposed her to pornography while he had lived with us in my old apartment. They said that any additional information would need to be reported to the detective and that he would communicate the details with me.

I remember feeling even worse than I did before. The guilt was overwhelming. I felt like it was my fault—I was the one who had moved them here, invited this monster into my life and the lives of my kids, and even had him babysit them for me. My mind raced with all kinds of scenarios. I wanted to know how I hadn't recognized any signs. I began to question myself about everything: Should I have asked more questions? Should I have paid closer attention? What could I have done to prevent this?

The children and I went back to the car, and I tried to figure out where the kids and I would go from there. After all, we were staying at my mom's place, and I knew my brother was still there. Being in that house was not an option. I called another brother and asked him if we could crash there for a few days until I figured out what to do. I contacted my mom and told her that we were not going to stay there while he was still there. The detective had to do his own investigation before any action could be taken legally, and I knew that the legal system took time. Of course I was not comfortable staying there with the kids while this process was being carried out.

My mother informed me that, while we were out, he had finally admitted to her what had been taking place with my daughter, and he had actually turned himself in at the police station. Regardless, I felt that the trauma of what had happened to my daughter was too fresh and overwhelming for us to even imagine staying in the home, at least for a while.

We went back to the house to get some of our belongings, then stayed at my other brother's house with his family. By this time, news of what had happened had spread like wildfire through my family. Of course, there were mixed feelings, including utter disbelief, anger, and resentment. Regardless of others' opinions, I knew in my heart that I had done what had needed to be done to, first and foremost, protect my daughter and, secondly, to make him accountable for his actions. Up to this point in my family, no one had ever been held accountable.

At the time, it didn't dawn on me that I was breaking this cycle, and I was even unsure of how far back into our family lineage it went. But I knew for certain that I wasn't going to allow it to continue with my children and family. I knew that I needed to take a stand and finally get justice for my daughter rather than turning a blind eye to the crime and thereby allowing yet another molester to get away with hurting yet another member of my family. I wanted this generational curse to end!

When I arrived at my mom's house, she told me how my brother confessed to her and how he was in tears and said that he didn't know what had happened to him to make him behave that way. She then told me the events that had taken place with my grandfather when she was young and how he would do the same things to her. She went into detail about the events and explained to me that he stopped right before she hit puberty so that he didn't risk getting her pregnant, as I mentioned earlier. Bear in mind, this was the first time I had heard this admission about my grandfather. I loved him deeply and had even relocated to help her with him. I felt betrayed, lied to, and unprotected, as he had been around me and my siblings our entire childhood. No one had ever told us what happened or even attempted to protect us from him doing the same thing to us. At this point, he was already deceased, so there was no way for me to be certain that he hadn't tried anything with me or my other siblings that I had mentally blocked out of my mind. I was devastated by this news; however, my compassion for her experience overshadowed my questions and concerns about myself.

I finally felt compelled to admit to her the events of my past molestation with my uncle, and I told her of the experience I'd had when God had revealed to me that my great-uncle was my sister's father. I'll never forget the look of shock and horror on her face when I revealed that I knew what had transpired. She hesitantly asked me who had told my sister, and I explained that it had happened when my best friend and sisters had been in town for my graduation from getting my master's degrees. She broke down and cried, sharing with me how my great-uncle would sodomize her and never attempted to penetrate her vaginally because he knew that would leave proof of his disgusting acts. However, he would still ejaculate in her, and as a result, she became pregnant while her hymen was still intact at the age of fifteen. She lied to her parents and told them that she was raped by a stranger, and my grandmother, who passed away when I was a year old, never knew the truth before she died. I began to break down and cry at her experience and, even more, the fact that she had lived with this secret for more years than I had been alive. It was the most overwhelming day of my life.

The events of what happened to her were almost too much to fathom because she was ridiculed and made out to be a liar by my family for all those years, not realizing what trauma she had to endure. I was even more devastated by the fact that my mother had to deliver my sister at the age of fifteen while still anatomically a virgin due to the fact that her hymen was still intact. I literally remember feeling sick to my stomach. I knew I could not mentally handle any more at that point. It was as though my entire life had been a lie: the elders of my family were a bunch of liars and terrible people who had allowed this vicious cycle to continue with innocent children over and over again, and no one had ever done anything about it.

I did not realize at the time, but God was going to use this experience with my daughter to bring closure and healing for my entire family. After what I learned, I knew my life and my family's lives would be forever changed. It was like the rug was pulled from under me and my family in an instant. I had no idea what was going to happen with my daughter's case or even how to handle the information I'd learned, but I knew that I had to be the change my family needed. I didn't know how to navigate through all of this, but I knew for sure that I didn't want another child in my family to experience this type of trauma and that the cycle had to end.

— CHAPTER 8 —

Getting Justice Using the Legal System

As mentioned in the previous chapter, without hesitation, I decided to take a stand and seek justice for my daughter. This process was devastating and sent both me and my family into a very dark place. Before I go into additional detail regarding the events that took place leading up to and during the trial, I want to make it clear that taking these steps to fight for my daughter took me to one of my deepest times of depression and anxiety. I was very fortunate to have a doctor who, despite my initial desire not to take medication for depression, took the events of my life into consideration and immediately had me complete a questionnaire that determined the depth of my depression and anxiety. Since it was so severe, I allowed her to prescribe me medication that, along with continuing weekly therapy for myself and the children, helped me to overcome the depression and anxiety.

The level of guilt and shame I felt for allowing my child to be placed in a situation for this to happen to her was unbearable to the point where I struggled to get out of bed. I would cry uncontrollably for weeks. I feel the need to mention this part of my journey because I want to encourage anyone reading this who may end up having to be the change in their family, bearing the responsibility of breaking the generational curse over their family, to recognize that this is a very heavy burden and will take an unimaginable amount of courage and strength. And please be prepared for how your family will react when you decide to take this stand. It could potentially cause you to never speak to some of your loved ones for the rest of your life. You have to be willing to take a stand no matter what the cost.

This journey to date was one of the most difficult things I've had to face, even in comparison to having a stillbirth when nine months pregnant and having a brother brutally murdered. This still trumped all of that trauma for me. Not only did I have to watch my daughter be forced to relive her trauma over and over again while being interviewed and interrogated, but I also had to watch her go through physical exams. Also, because this abuse happened in two different counties, she had to go through some of this twice.

I was contacted by a detective in the SVU the day after we reported the incident. He and a female partner had me go back to my mom's house so they could collect any DNA evidence and take pictures of the living space in the basement where the incident had occurred. By this time, my brother had turned himself in to the police and was in the local jail awaiting a hearing. According to the detectives, they did not want interview him before collecting physical evidence. I spoke with the detectives after the samples were collected, which included her clothing and bedsheets. They made me aware that they found panties behind his bed that belonged to both me and my daughter that he was likely ejaculating into. This was extremely disturbing, as I was still in shock that I had never picked up on that vibe from him. He and I were very close, and I would've never imagined these things about him.

The detectives assured me that they would keep me posted on all of the details regarding the case as it progressed and what the next steps would be after the interview. I eventually heard back from the detectives that he fully admitted to the sexual abuse that had occurred in both my mom's house and my home.

I hadn't realized that the abuse had been going on for several years right under my nose, and my daughter never told me. I know that it is not unusual for children to keep these things a secret, but I had purposely talked to my children about sexual abuse as early as they were able to identify their body parts. I always told my children to tell me if anyone touched them inappropriately and assured them that they would not be ignored and never had to feel guilty or afraid of telling. I could not shake the feeling of myself failing as a mother.

Additionally, the detectives informed me of other disturbing details regarding the molestation. They assured me that since they had a confession, the next steps would be much simpler than if we had not had a confession. They informed me that I would be visited by someone from child protective services to conduct a separate investigation. Because I was staying at my other brother's home at the time, they would have to do a home visit and ensure that my children were not in any danger in his home.

After a while, I had the home visit with the case worker from child protective services and was contacted by the detective every step of the way to see how we were holding up. He was an angel who took this case personally as if it were his own child. He was very attentive and checked on us through the process.

Once the CPS investigation was concluded, I was instructed to file a protective order against my brother just in case something happened and he was released. I filed the emergency protective order and was awarded it. A trial date was set for the permanent protective order while the emergency order was placed in effect.

In the meantime, I waited for what seemed like an eternity for my brother's arraignment. This was the day I dreaded because it would be the first time I would see him since the incident, and I was not sure how I was going to conduct myself in court. I didn't know what reaction I would have, but I knew that it was not going to be easy. So many emotions rushed in at once: anger, hurt, rage, feeling triggered because of my past trauma, and much more. I was so emotionally all over the place that I didn't know what to anticipate. The detective supported me every step of the way, ensuring me that neither me nor my child would have to attend the arraignment, but I knew I had to be there to look him in the eye.

That dreaded day finally arrived. The courtroom was extremely crowded. There were all kinds of cases being heard in this courtroom, criminal cases mostly, but I remember immediately feeling guilt and shame that I would have to hear the charges being announced in a room full of strangers. I was embarrassed and even wanted to give up because of the shame, but I knew that I had to press forward and take a stand to look him in the eye.

However, because of the nature of the charges, and to protect him from other inmates harming him, his charges were not announced in the arraignment until after everyone else's charges were announced. His attorney had requested his case be heard last for his protection. I remember feeling angry that he was being protected by his attorney and questioning where the protection was for the victim.

I sat in the courtroom for a long time and heard murderers, drug dealers, and repeat offenders get awarded bail. The process of listening to all the charges against the people in court didn't help me trust our legal system, because it didn't seem like the people accused of such terrible crimes were getting anything more than a slap on the wrist. Toward the middle of hearing the cases, the state's attorney informed me that his arraignment would be conducted via video conferencing and not face-to-face as I had expected. I have to be honest, as much I wanted to face him, I don't think I was mentally strong enough to look at him face-to-face. The video conference proved to be the easier way to deal with this situation.

The time finally arrived for his case to be called before the judge. We were the last people in the courtroom at this point. His charges were read, and I began to weep. It was the first time I had heard anyone other than the detectives list all the charges being brought against him. The detective told me that they would focus on the charges that carried the maximum sentencing for him, but that some of the charges would likely be dropped due to the way the legal system worked. He assured me that he would make sure that the evidence he collected as well as my testimony, the testimony from my daughter, and his confession would result in getting the charges with the harshest sentencing to stick.

On the TV screen, they called my brother into the room, and I saw him shackled and in handcuffs with his head down. It made me cry uncontrollably, thinking, *How did we get here? What made him do such horrific things?* I even wondered if I'd noticed any signs before and had maybe just ignored them. The overwhelming flood of thoughts was almost unbearable. The charges against him that hadn't been dropped were read, and his attorney asked for bail. My attorney fought for him to stay in jail until his hearing due to the nature of the charges and the fact that we technically lived in the home where the events had occurred. My attorney also mentioned that there was a protective order put in place. Despite his attorney pleading that he had no criminal record, the judge was very clear that it was best for him not to be awarded bail due to the nature of the charges.

He was then taken away in handcuffs and shackles. I remember thinking that I should've felt a sense of relief, but in actuality, I felt even worse. The reality and severity of what was happening was beginning to sink in.

This was the beginning of the journey to getting justice for my daughter. When we left the court, I received a call from the lead detective letting me know that the attorney who was at the pre-trial hearing would not be the regular attorney assigned to the case and that we would have to be patient because this process was likely going to take several months.

— CHAPTER 9 —

The Legal Process Continued

It took months for the legal system to process the trial, and prior to the trial for the first county in which he was accused, I had to appear in court for the final order of protection to be put into place. I felt really nervous, not knowing whether my daughter would need to be present or if I had to see him since the arraignment had been done via video conferencing. The state's attorney's office confirmed that she would not need to be present, which offered me my first sense of relief.

When I entered the courtroom, I remember feeling the sense of shame overwhelm me yet again, as the courtroom was full of people. I knew that everyone was there for various reasons, some severe and some not severe, but all I could think about was how much I didn't want to talk about the circumstances that had led up to this point. I also feared that I would see people I knew who would then be aware of all of my family's personal business. Despite all of this fear and anxiety, I knew that what I needed to do was far more important than any of my fears and was necessary to ensure that my daughter received the justice she deserved. I also recalled that morning after my graduation when I had learned the truth about my sister's father, and I knew this cycle had to end for my entire family. I knew what needed to be done and why I needed to do it, but it didn't make the journey any easier.

After sitting through many other cases, I looked straight ahead and saw my brother come into the courtroom in shackles and handcuffs. Immediately, I was overwhelmed with pain, and I burst into tears. I am usually pretty calm, cool, and collected under pressure, but I guess all of the emotions flooded in at one time, and I was overwhelmed. I knew that once he was seated in the courtroom, I had to get my emotions under control and face him. As my name was called and I began walking to the plaintiff's area of the courtroom, I told myself that I had nothing to be ashamed of and that I needed to look him in his eyes while I pled my case for this permanent order of protection.

I approached the front of the courtroom, and the judge began to read out the charges. When it was my time to speak, I held my head high and told the judge the events that had occurred and why I felt that the permanent order of protection was necessary, just in case he was released for any reason. The judge gave him the opportunity to speak, and he said he wanted to leave this state anyway after his release and that he would not be around us. I was more upset at his attitude than I was any other time prior. He was acting smug, as if he didn't have any remorse for his actions. Regardless of how angry and upset I was, I was mindful to keep my composure. The judge then granted me the permanent order of protection for my mother's home, my daughter's school, aftercare, and any common places where we would be.

After the order was awarded, I was told to go to another part of the building to get a copy of the protection order. I reminded myself that the steps I was taking to get and seek justice were necessary, and based on his behavior in the courtroom, he did not feel remorse for what he did. I prayed as I returned home for God to give me the strength to keep going through this process and to keep my eyes focused on why I needed to do this.

Several months went by, and things were quiet on the legal front for a while. The case was postponed several times, which is not unusual. I continued therapy for myself and my children, and we were starting to get back to a semi-regular routine. Finally, I received a call from the state's attorney asking us to come into their office so that my daughter could be prepped for testimony. This made my heart drop to my stomach because the last thing I wanted was for her to relive this tragedy, but I knew this was a possibility if they felt her recorded interviews were not enough. The worst part was having to break the news to my daughter that this was something she would potentially need to do. When I got home, I sat my children down and told them that she may have to testify in open court if his attorney pushed the issue and that she would have to recount the events again. We were all devastated, but I explained to them that the only way we could make him take responsibility for his actions was to continue with this case and that we would be protecting anyone else from going through this by taking this step.

To my surprise, my daughter understood why this was necessary. We went to the district attorney's office, and I was amazed at how much compassion he had for my family. He assured me that he would do everything in his power to prevent her from testifying, but he wanted to prepare us just in case. He was extremely gentle and kind with us. He and his assistant met with me first, and then they took my daughter to a different room to prepare her for the hearing. After about an hour, the attorney informed me that she did well and was able to clearly explain the events that had happened just as she had in her initial interview. This gave me a sense of relief, but I still did not want her to be forced to take the stand and be cross-examined by his attorney. I felt like the entire process would make her feel like a victim all over again.

I was pleasantly surprised to find out, a few days later, that my attorney and my brother's attorney agreed that she would not need to testify and that my attorney would read out loud a transcript of her testimony in court. My attorney also informed me that they were able to reach a plea deal.

I have to rewind for a moment. A few weeks prior, I firmly told my attorney that I wanted the most severe charges that carried the maximum number of years to be given to him. I did not want him to receive a slap on the wrist. I wanted my daughter to get justice and for him to pay for what he did. When my attorney informed me of the plea deal, he knew that I would be willing to go to trial if my brother did not serve a fair amount of time for his crimes. After all was said and done, the nine or so charges were reduced to only two charges, which together carried a maximum sentence of twenty-five years. While I was well aware that most rapists don't serve twenty-five years in prison, I knew that he would be put away for a long time.

We finally reached the day of the hearing. My sister flew in from out of town to support me. She stood with me the entire day. Initially, we arrived at the witness room, and despite being told of the plea deal, I still needed to be prepared to go to court in case anything went awry. My sister and I stood in the building where witnesses are held for several hours. I felt extremely calm and focused, as I knew that, once I completed this hearing, we could start to heal as a family. I knew that us taking this stand to fight for justice would make anyone else in the family who wanted to sexually abuse yet another person think twice. I wanted this to be the end of the curse of molestation and incest for my family once and for all.

My sister and I were informed that it was time for us to head over to the courtroom because my brother had just arrived. It was almost time for our case to be heard. We were escorted by a court officer to a bench in the middle of a crowded courtroom where there was standing room only. For the first time that day, I began to feel a sense of fear, anxiety, and shame come over me. This time it wasn't just for my daughter: it also dredged up memories of my own trauma and made me feel overwhelmed. I began to weep silently, and my leg shook uncontrollably as I sat on the bench with all of the other people waiting to hear their cases. My sister looked at me and said, "You are doing something for our family that no one was ever bold enough to do, and you can do this." I looked at her, the direct result of incest in our family, and knew that I was not only getting justice for my daughter that day, but I was getting justice for myself, my sister, my mother, and anyone else who had been through this in generations past. In that very moment, I knew I was the voice for all of us who had been silenced for years and who had been forced to live with this secret.

The dreaded time was upon us. My brother was escorted to the defendant's area in shackles and handcuffs where his attorney awaited him as the judge called us to the front of the courtroom. As I was walking toward the stand, the charges were being read out loud, and you could almost hear a pin drop, the courtroom was so quiet. Some people said out loud, "Oh my God." And a lady behind me said, "I have to go. I can't stay in this courtroom and hear this case."

At that moment, I knew that the road ahead of me was going to be tough, but I knew I could do it. My attorney asked the judge if my sister could stand next to me for moral support, and she allowed it. She held my hand as we moved to the plaintiff's side of the bench. The judge asked how my brother pleaded, and he said, "Guilty." My attorney began to read off the transcript of the testimony taken from my daughter when she was interviewed and began to detail all of the events that occurred. I looked over at my brother, who held his head down the entire time, and began to weep. The judge then asked me if I had prepared a statement or if there was anything that I needed to add. I then spoke of how my brother had used the love that my daughter and I had for him against us and how he had taken her innocence away from her. I mentioned how I had gone out of my way to help him find employment and get on his feet financially, and instead of showing gratitude, he had taken advantage of our love and trust and used his power of influence to abuse and intimidate my child. I even mentioned that my brother knew what his father had done to me and how it had affected me. And to think that he could do this to his niece, who called him her favorite uncle, made him worse than a rapist off the street.

Once I finished my testimony, the judge asked him if he had anything to say, and he declined. His attorney then petitioned the court to have him receive therapy while he served his time. My attorney and I agreed that this would be best for him. The judge made sure that he understood the terms of the plea deal and asked if he had any questions or objections. He said that he understood, and his sentence was read. He was to get credit for time served, which at this point was about six months, and he would have to serve at least ten years of his twenty-five year sentence without the possibility of parole.

I walked out of that courtroom like a weight had been temporarily removed from my shoulders. We still had to deal with the second case in the other jurisdiction, so it was not over yet. At least I knew what the process was like, and I knew that the second case would be very similar to the first.

A few months later, I met with the state's attorney to prepare for the other case. I was told that I would be interviewed again regarding the events that occurred at my old place, and they would likely attempt to have the same deal in that county as in the first county. Since he had confessed to the events that occurred at my old apartment and I had not had knowledge of the events prior to his confession, they would likely use the confession and her testimony as the evidence needed to convict him in that county.

The second case was much easier because the same plea deal was given. My brother was given concurrent sentences, which meant that he would serve no more than twenty years and wouldn't be eligible for parole until after serving at least ten years.

While the prospect of him serving ten years in prison is not even remotely equivalent to the lifetime of healing that my daughter and my family will have, it is still refreshing that, for the first time in our family's history, someone is paying for the curse of incest and sexual assault within our family.

— CHAPTER 10 —

The Beginning of the Healing Process

As I mentioned in the earlier chapters, I am not really sure how far the history of incest, rape, molestation, and sexual assault dates back for my family, but one thing is for sure, I know that the cycle of keeping these acts a secret ended on the day I decided to take a stand and make my brother pay for his actions. While he most certainly wasn't the first perpetrator, he definitely was the last who would ever be emboldened enough to try it without thinking of the consequences that would follow. I truly believe this curse is broken for good from this generation and any future generations to come.

One of the remarkable things that came out of this entire process was the fact that my sister, who had been born as a result of incest, decided to call a family meeting with all of the family members as far back as great-uncles and aunts and confront everyone about the secrets and how they were the cause of this cycle continuing. My sister and I rounded up everyone either on video chat, three-way call, or face-to-face to meet about this subject. Because we didn't want to keep pressuring my mother to relive the trauma of her experiences, we knew that what happened needed to be put out in the open. We gathered at a central location. We did not inform the family what the meeting would be about, because we knew that some would try to avoid it or just not show up. We ensured that all of my siblings were either there in person or on the phone, that my aunts and uncles all joined either by phone or video chat, and that the great-aunts and uncles who were not deceased were available. We also ensured that the older nieces and nephews were in attendance (those who were of age to understand the conversation being had).

Once we gathered everyone together, my sister spoke first and informed everyone of what had happened with my brother and how the knowledge of this event had led to revealing the secret of my great-uncle repeatedly raping, violating, and sexually assaulting my mother. She also boldly revealed that my mom, after all these years, admitted to her that he was her father. She also revealed the sexual abuse that my mother had sustained at the hand of my grandfather, who was deceased. My great-aunt, who was one of the few living relatives of that generation, said she had no idea that her brother was the one who had done this to my mom and was my sister's father.

It was an extremely heavy and emotional conversation, but it was definitely necessary. Everyone in the meeting had a chance to speak and share, and we made sure that everyone had the chance to inform us all of any other abuse that we may not have been aware of. This meeting was the first time our family ever spoke candidly about the sexual abuse in the family and how we could do a better job of banding together to protect each other. In that moment, the veil of shame, fear, and hurt was lifted, and all masks were removed.

This was the moment that I actually felt our family come back together as a unit. There were many tears, prayers, and promises of accountability shared during that meeting. I remember embracing my mother and weeping for her. I felt that, for the first time, she actually got justice and her voice was heard—not through her speaking at the meeting, but because she was finally able to stop holding a forty-year-old secret. She could finally stop feeling ostracized and whispered about because she could finally live freely in the truth of what had happened to her as a victim and no longer be viewed as if she had done something wrong. I had not anticipated that this one act of standing up and making someone pay for their crimes would bring to light years and generations of secrets that were hidden for so long and, with that, bring healing.

In this chapter, I want to encourage anyone who is going through similar issues with sexual abuse, incest, or molestation of any kind to learn practical steps to heal and recover from the effects of this type of trauma. Many talk about healing but don't know how to heal or even where to begin. But before I mention the practical steps to healing, I want to mention some of the signs that victims of sexual assault often have. My prayer is that knowing what signs to look for could help family members become more vigilant and aware of what could be happening to their loved ones.

According to Bridges, a nonprofit created as resources for victims of domestic and sexual assault, some of the signs that can indicate that children and adolescents are or have been victims of sexual assault are included below.

Behavioral Indicators in Younger Children:
- Bed wetting
- Fecal soiling
- Eating problems (overeating, under eating)

- Fears or phobias
- Overly compulsive behavior
- School problems or significant change in school performance (attitude and grades)
- Regression to behavior already mastered, such as thumb sucking, bed-wetting, etc.
- Inability to concentrate
- Sleep disturbances (e.g., nightmares, fearful about falling asleep, fretful sleep patterns, or sleeping long hours)

Behavioral Indicators in Older Children and Adolescents:
- Withdrawal from family, friends, or usual activities
- Depression or anxiety
- Passive or overly pleasing behavior
- Poor hygiene or excessive bathing
- Poor peer relations and social skills
- Acting out, running away or aggressive behavior
- Alcohol or drug abuse
- School problems, frequent absences, sudden drop in school performance
- Refusal to dress for physical education
- Nonparticipation in sports and social activities
- Fearful of showers/restrooms
- Fearful of home life demonstrated by arriving at school early or leaving late
- Suddenly fearful of other things (e.g., going outside, participating in familiar activities)

- Extraordinary fear of males (of being approached or touched by them)
- Self-consciousness of body beyond that expected for age
- Crying without provocation
- Suicide attempts

If you notice any of these signs or symptoms displayed, be willing to have a conversation and create a nonjudgmental and safe space for the potential victim to talk. If it is confirmed that they are a victim of sexual assault, be willing to help them find resources in their area.

I want to now discuss some of the practical steps that I took and am currently taking to heal and to help my family heal. One of the first practical steps I took was therapy. As I mentioned, I started therapy years ago. I knew that when I relocated after my divorce, I needed therapy to continue to cope with the divorce and managing my life as a single mother, and also to heal from my own childhood traumas. As I mentioned, my trauma did not just include sexual abuse, but also abandonment, domestic violence, alcoholism, extreme poverty, and other issues that started as early as I can remember. When I look back on my decision to continue therapy after my relocation, I did not imagine it would be more valuable than I had expected from the beginning. After being confronted with the trauma that my daughter experienced, it triggered some memories of my own trauma that I had not felt or remembered for years.

I also want to add that I had my doctor prescribe me antidepressants. I knew that I needed them because I literally could not go one day without crying and feeling an overwhelming sense of guilt and despair. While I am not suggesting that everyone needs to be prescribed medication, I am saying that if you feel as though you can't get through this process without it, don't be afraid to be honest with yourself and your doctor about the best course of action.

I didn't know that these events would lead not only to my healing, but also to the healing for generations before me. I always ask myself why God chose to use me to bring about healing for my family and to break this curse. And, without fail, every time I ask that question, I feel in my heart God telling me that it was not that I was so special; he just knew that I would be bold enough and strong enough to do it.

I sincerely want anyone who reads this book to know that you don't have to be the oldest, youngest, richest, or any of those factors. God just wants someone who will be willing to do what is necessary when needed. I'm no more special than anyone else; I just have such a hate for injustice that he knew I would speak up and take the action needed to ensure justice was served. I encourage you, reader, to do the same! You have strength that you do not know you possess to make a difference and break the curse over your family as well.

The second practical step to healing is learning to forgive yourself and the perpetrator who hurt you. This is the most difficult but necessary step in the healing process. I will never forget when I was struggling, years ago, with forgiving my first husband for his infidelity. I was in church during one Bible study or Sunday service, and my pastor said something that I remember to this day and will likely never forget. He said, "Forgiveness is a decision and not a feeling." He said we must choose to forgive, and when we feel negative thoughts come up in our minds about what that person did to us or how they wronged us, we must say out loud, "I set my will to forgive." That principle stuck with me then, and I live by and practice it today. It helped me to release the unforgiveness and bitterness toward my ex-husband as well as my perpetrators. I will be the first to admit that it is one of the hardest things to do, but we have a responsibility to protect ourselves and our hearts from bitterness. What many fail to realize is that when you hold on to unforgiveness, you actually harm your own physical and mental health while the perpetrator who did you wrong gets to walk around free. You must not give anyone the power to control your life, and forgiveness is the first way you can take your power and life back into your own hands.

I feel in my spirit that I must mention this point: forgiveness does not mean that you allow a person to continue to stay in your life, nor does it mean that you have to ever talk to that person again. You can forgive that person and still choose to protect yourself from them forever. This may mean cutting them completely out of your life.

In the situation with my brother and my uncle who abused me, I will never speak to them again, but I made peace in my heart with them. I refused to let unforgiveness, bitterness, hurt, and resentment ravage me like cancer. Because my brother broke my trust and violated both me and my children in ways that would make me unable to trust him, I knew that the trust was forever destroyed. While I may never say a word to him again, I prayed for him that God would help him be free of the demons that he allowed himself to be open to. I was also told that he, too, was a victim of sexual assault in his earlier years but had never admitted it to anyone until this case was brought to light. I now pray sincerely for God to heal him and set him free. I pray that during his time in prison he renews his relationship with God and is delivered.

The third practical step that I suggest implementing is taking the time to use your pain to help someone else who is dealing with similar pain. I know that I said the previous step was the most important, but this one is probably neck and neck when it comes to importance.

Throughout this process of living through the most painful trauma I've experienced in my life, I had already realized that I was called to be a life coach. But what I did not know was that God would use this experience to help me give birth to Overcoming Abuse Through Healing, Inc. (OATH). I started this nonprofit as my way of giving back to the community and providing a safe space for people who are dealing with various forms of trauma to attend, share, and heal. To date, this is one of my greatest and most precious pursuits. While everyone's way of giving back may vary, it is very important to understand that in order to heal fully, you should be willing to be open and vulnerable about your journey because you never know how much your story will impact the lives of others.

In addition to the nonprofit, I am also a certified life coach. While many who know me closely call me "Pastor E," I always laugh because, while I don't feel called or qualified to be a pastor, I definitely have a heart and passion for helping people heal and reach their highest potential. I honestly love that I can help uplift people in the space where I am without the "religious" dynamic. I am far from a religious person, but my relationship with God is real and sincere, and I just want to make a difference and empower others to heal and be victorious.

The next step to healing and recovering is to remember that healing is a lifelong journey. I think we put so much pressure on ourselves to get it right every time and hope that healing is something we do to overcome that hurt, and then once we've done the work, the healing is over and done. This is not the case, especially when overcoming such a devastating event such as sexual abuse. This healing journey has ups and downs, ebbs and flows. What I have learned over the course of this healing process is that your decision to be healed and whole requires daily and intentional work. For example, you can be in a relationship and have a random argument, and based on what the other person says to you, you could find yourself being triggered. Another example: someone who was violently raped could find themselves triggered if someone walks up behind them too closely. Seemingly random and unrelated incidents could ultimately lead to someone being triggered. These examples may seem far-fetched, but oftentimes, we are living in fight-or-flight mode without even realizing it, and in a moment's notice, something could cause us to snap.

This is why I am a firm believer in taking practical and intentional steps to maintain our mental health and heal on a daily basis. While I am not a licensed therapist or doctor, I understand that every human walking this planet has had some form of trauma that has shaped the way they view the world and how they respond to others in society. A prime example would be a woman who has abandonment issues, such as myself, being drawn to men who need fixing. Because of my trauma, I often found myself tied to and in relationships with people who were broken, and because of our trauma bond, I wanted to "fix" them. All this did for me was cause me pain, hurt, stress, and depression. It wasn't until I made the decision to make healing a lifelong journey that I realized I had this characteristic, then I was able to take steps to correct the behavior.

We must be real with ourselves at all times about where we are and why we have some of the behaviors we have. It is not until we take this action that we will be able to actually heal and be whole. When I think back to my own life and journey, I am still so far away from where I want to be, but I am so much more self-aware and patient with myself. I feel led to say, "Please don't beat yourself down with the words you speak about yourself while you're on this journey." We are often not kind to ourselves, especially when it comes to our words. I can recall many times beating myself up about how I chose the men I married and how I was stupid for allowing myself to be in those situations. What I did not realize was that every time I spoke those negative words and had those negative thoughts about myself, I was in essence speaking that curse over my life. We are the master of our own world based on the words we speak over ourselves. After realizing this fact, I began to speak kindly about myself and speak words that brought healing and empowerment and were uplifting. Now I am much more conscious of the words I speak over myself and others, so when I catch myself speaking negatively, I quickly correct it and speak something positive to combat the negative self-talk.

My final step to healing is to start doing things that you enjoy, and begin to live and love life again. Just because you were raped, abused, or victimized doesn't mean you have to stay stuck in that mental space. You owe it to yourself to lead a normal, happy, and healthy life. My honest belief is that every human was put on this earth for two reasons: to love and to be loved. No matter how young or old you were when you were victimized, you must understand that God's best is for you to be happy and healthy, mentally, physically, emotionally, and financially.

In order to achieve this step, you should be intentional. You can start this process by surrounding yourself with people who genuinely love and care for you. Next, figure out what hobbies you would like to explore or what things you enjoy, and purposely make doing those things a part of your daily or weekly routine. For example, when I broke up with a guy that I really loved, instead of staying home on Saturday nights being bored, I started taking myself out on dates. This was truly a turning point for me because I was quickly able to move past the feelings of hurt, loneliness, and pain and start enjoying spending time with myself and getting to know myself. This turning point led me to my life coaching journey.

The practical steps that I have given you are just the beginning. I honestly think that finding a good therapist and taking a more practical and intentional approach to healing is needed. We can ultimately determine whether we want to be a victim or be victorious. Despite my many challenges in the journey called life, I never looked at myself as a victim. I was able to learn something from all of these challenges rather than letting the challenges define me. I made a decision a long time ago not to give anyone who hurt me, abused me, or harmed me power to control my future. I knew I had to take my power back and never allow another human being to have the authority to determine my outcome in life. That downright stubbornness of my fixed nature refuses to give someone the power to control me in that way.

As I mentioned in the very beginning of this book, the purpose of this book is not to hurt anyone or cause shame or pain. I wrote this book as a tool to help bring healing to families and victims of sexual abuse. It's unfortunate that my journey is not unusual or unique because the issue of rape, incest, molestation, and sexual assault happens in many families. I would venture to say that this issue is extremely common and, unfortunately, continues to happen because people are too ashamed and too deeply hurt, and they would rather bury the issue than deal with it and begin the process of healing on the road to recovery. I want to rid the world of victim shaming, and I want to bring to light that keeping such acts a secret in the family perpetuates the cycle. Instead of providing protection for the family, it actually has the opposite effect and causes the perpetrators to think that they can get away with it. We must understand that the secret keeping is the reason most pedophiles and rapists can continue to victimize, because they have no fear of the consequences of their actions. Unfortunately, the victims are often the people who end up feeling the shame and fear while the perpetrators are free to continue victimizing.

I want this book to empower people to the point where pedophiles, rapists, and molesters will think twice before preying on people for fear of being exposed and made to pay for their actions. My sincere desire is to bring healing and eradicate this issue within the family. I desire for this book to reach millions and give victims a voice to stand up and decide that they are no longer going to allow the acts of sexual immorality to plague their families. It is also my sincere prayer that people transition from being victims to being victorious and overcomers who will never allow what happened to them to define them.

As I started this journey of telling my story, I knew that this was something I had to do. I no longer wanted to tolerate the pain and damage that the acts caused my family. I am sure there will be family members who won't understand why I chose to discuss these topics. For me, the answer is simple—I felt led to expose this issue so that others can learn that they can heal and lead a successful life despite the circumstances that occurred. Additionally, I want to give a voice to those who were victimized and felt that no one else understood or could imagine their journey. I encourage and challenge those who have experienced this type of trauma to sit down and have open dialogues in their family so that the family unit can begin the process and journey to healing. In my humble opinion, this is the only way the family will begin to support one another and continue the healing process. I will say it again, I believe that the keeping of these secrets is why it has been able to continue for generations. When someone stands up and speaks on the issue, then and only then will people's awareness and knowledge of potential signs be made clear to the family. I know that this book focused mainly on incest and sexual abuse in the family unit, but some of the same warning signs can appear in those who were violated sexually by a complete stranger. I want this book to serve as a guide to parents who may have difficulty discussing these issues with their children and for children to gain the courage and strength to tell. I want these words to serve as healing and minister to all who read them.

According to The Rape, Abuse & Incest National Network (RAINN), there are several ways to have conversations about sexual assault with children starting at an early age. Some of the tips given include the following:

- **Teach children the names of their body parts.** When children have the words to describe their body parts, they may find it easier to ask questions and express concerns about those body parts.

- **Some parts of the body are private.** Let children know that other people shouldn't touch or look at them. If a healthcare professional has to examine these parts of the body, be present.

- **It's OK to say "no."** It's important to let children know they are allowed to say "no" to touches that make them uncomfortable. This message isn't obvious to children, who are often taught to be obedient and follow the rules. Support your child if they say no, even if it puts you in an uncomfortable position. For example, if your child doesn't want to hug someone at a family gathering, respect their decision to say "no" to this contact.

- **Talk about secrets.** Perpetrators will often use secret-keeping to manipulate children. Let children know they can always talk to you, especially if they've been told to keep a secret. If they see someone touching another child, they shouldn't keep this secret, either. Learn more about **protecting a child from sexual assault**.

- **Reassure them that they won't get in trouble.** Young children often fear getting in trouble or upsetting their parents by asking questions or talking about their experiences. Be a safe place for your child to share information about things that they have questions about or that make them uncomfortable. Remind them they won't be punished for sharing this information with you.

- **Show them what it looks like to do the right thing.** It could be as simple as helping an elderly person get off a bus or picking up change that someone has dropped on the ground. When you model helping behavior it signals to your child that this is a normal, positive way to behave.

- **When they come to you, make time for them.** If your kid comes to you with something they feel is important, take the time to listen. Give them your undivided attention, and let them know you take their concerns seriously. They may be more likely to come to you in the future if they know their voice will be heard.

My final message is to the predators. I pray that you get delivered from the demons you battle and seek help rather than cause your potential future victims to take a lifetime to heal from your actions and the pain you caused. God is far more loving and compassionate than I will ever be, but I honestly want you to get some help and ask God to remove that negative behavior and warped mindset from you. God's love for mankind reaches far beyond what my brain and heart can comprehend, and only he knows how to heal you. I also want to say to the perpetrators that I know that many of you, too, were victims of sexual assault. I am very aware of the old saying that hurting people hurt people; however, this is not an excuse to cause the same type of pain and devastation to someone else. Rather than continuing the cycle, you have the power to break the cycle and get healing and justice for your experiences.

You must understand that the only way to overcome this cycle is to change it. You must begin to be honest with yourself and seek help immediately to get assistance with dealing with your pain. For once, put yourself in the same position as your victim. You remember how devastating it felt to be put in that predicament when it was happening to you, so why would you want someone else to feel that same pain? I often feel that people who struggle with these urges don't take the time to be honest with a therapist, counselor, or pastor about these urges, so rather than trying to get help, they just succumb to their lustful desires. If you really want to change, it is possible. There is a way out if you just take the necessary steps to overcome.

As I bring my story to a close, I want to again thank all of my family members who graciously gave me permission to tell their story to show how the generational curse plagued so many of them. I want you all to know that I love you with a deeper love than I have the words to express, and I am looking forward to the healing that our family has begun to experience and for the continued healing in our future. For the family members who did not want to see these truths come out, I pray you understand my heart and why I had to expose the pain in order for us to heal. I want nothing but God's best for each of you. I pray that the love and healing we experience as a family will supersede any pain and trauma that we experienced. I am especially grateful to all of those who have been there as a support for us, for all the pastors, therapists, counselors, attorneys, and friends who have helped my family to overcome. As we all go through this journey, may we all experience God's absolute best, and may restoration and peace be our new story.

Last, and certainly not least, I want to thank each and every person who, because of the stories shared in this book, will have the courage and strength to heal and overcome the generational curse of incest and molestation in their family. This journey is far from easy, and, because of the deep shame and being forced to reopen buried wounds, many are unable to take this journey. While I am sure there are stories that are far worse and even more devastating than my own or those of my family members, this journey takes an immense amount of guts, courage, and strength. I want to encourage you to have open dialogues with your family members and be willing to get the justice you deserve should you so choose. Please know that I am praying with you for strength and wisdom to go through this process.

I also want you to understand that this journey will not have the support of all of your family members, friends, and loved ones, but one thing is for sure: you have the right to be healed and to face the truth, no matter how uncomfortable, if it means that you are able to bring about change in your family. I just want you to be prepared for potential backlash and slander and to know this: no one can silence you if you choose to tell your story and share your truth. I had to come to terms with the fact that this book will make some never speak to me, some hate me, and some be embarrassed. My heart is that we speak candidly about these generational curses in order to bring healing and future generational blessings. May God richly bless each and every person who is inspired, touched, compelled, and healed as a result of this story. I love you all with the true love of God and can't wait to hear of the testimonies and breakthroughs that will come to all who read this book.

www.ingramcontent.com/pod-product-compliance
Lightning Source LLC
LaVergne TN
LVHW012252070526
838201LV00111B/336/J